THEORY INTO PRACTICE

146   This Issue: Transforming School Counseling

148   Transforming School Counseling: A National Perspective
Patricia J. Martin

154   Preparing School Counselors to Be Leaders and Advocates: A Critical Need in the New Millennium
Reese M. House and Susan Jones Sears

163   Recruiting Leaders to Transform School Counseling
Charles Hanson and Carolyn Stone

169   Transforming School Counselor Preparation Programs
Richard L. Hayes and Pamela O. Paisley

177   Inducting the Transformed School Counselor Into the Profession
C. Marie Jackson, Brent M. Snow, Susan R. Boes, Paul L. Phillips, Rebecca Powell Stanard, Linda C. Painter, and Mary Beth Wulff

186   The Transformed School Counselor in Action
Sue Musheno and Mary Talbert

192   Transforming the Rural School Counselor
Peggy LaTurno Hines

202   Additional Resources for Classroom Use

Guest Editor: Susan Jones Sears

Next Issue: Revising Bloom's Taxonomy

To celebrate our anniversary, the covers of the four 40th-anniversary issues carry the names of each contributor to *TIP* since 1962. As you examine the covers, you will see a veritable *Who's Who* of education. With this 40th-anniversary volume, we also introduce a new feature: "Additional Resources for Classroom Use." In addition to the article's references, each author has provided annotated bibliographies of periodicals, books, or Web sites that extend the content of the article and focus on the implications for practitioners.

This Issue

A CLOSE EXAMINATION OF educational practices in schools serving low-income and minority students reveals some disturbing trends: Low-income and minority students are most likely to be taught by the least skilled teachers. Their schools often have fewer instructional resources, including current textbooks and laboratory equipment. In a variety of ways the teachers, administrators, and counselors appear to hold low expectations for these students and, therefore, do not encourage them to schedule rigorous academic courses. In too many instances, students in high-poverty and high-minority schools see no connection between what is being taught and a better future for themselves. In some schools, however, low-income and minority students succeed at high levels despite the disadvantages. These are schools where students are held to high academic standards, pushed to achieve, and given support to learn. In these schools, there are significant adults who believe that disadvantaged students *can* succeed, and they create conditions conducive to student learning (Education Trust, 1999).

In the seventies and eighties, public education made tremendous progress in narrowing the achievement gap evident in high-minority and high-poverty schools; but since the end of the eighties, progress, with few exceptions, appears to have stopped (Education Trust, 1999). The United States cannot afford the human, economic, and civic costs associated with failing to provide all of its young people with the skills and knowledge they and the nation need to compete and thrive in this new century.

Concerned about the achievement gap, the DeWitt Wallace-Reader's Digest Fund has studied ways of eliminating it. In the early nineties, the Fund began to conduct research in the field of school counseling. Their findings convinced them that school counselors can and must play a role in improving schools and making them more equitable. The school counselor is the school professional in the best position to identify systemic and other barriers that impede students' academic success. Counselors are often aware of issues of equity and access, data about student achievement, reports of school failure, and community and family conditions. Unfortunately, school counselors have not systematically used this data to advocate for underserved students or to lead school reform.

A variety of reasons have been proposed to explain why many school counselors are not change agents. Some proponents of counseling suggest that the role of school counselors is determined by harried school administrators who draft counselors to do semi-administrative duties, such as preparing master class schedules or handling lunch duties. Another reason receiving increasing national attention is the preparation of school counselors. Many students spend hours in their graduate-level preparation programs learning how to counsel individual students as if they were ultimately going to deal primarily with the *social* and *personal* needs of young people. Thus, they do not learn how to intervene with students to improve their *academic achievement*. Nor do they learn how to advocate for students or push for needed changes in schools. In order to improve guidance counseling in public schools by transforming graduate-level preparation of counselors, the DeWitt Wallace Fund selected six universities to lead a national effort to reform the preparation of public school counselors. The universities, working with public school districts, along with the Education Trust, will share $3.5 million in grants from the Fund to make changes in graduate-level training programs. Known as the Transforming School Counseling Initiative (TSCI), the grant charged the Trust with producing a conceptual framework for changing school counseling preparation programs so future counselors can better serve elementary, middle, and high school students, especially those in low-income communities. The six universities taking part in the Fund's initiative include California State University-Northridge, Indiana State University, the State University of West Georgia, The Ohio State University, The University of Georgia, and the University of North Florida.

This special issue of *Theory Into Practice*, "Transforming School Counseling," describes the changes the TSCI is proposing and how these changes can affect the professional practice of school counseling. In the first article, Martin provides a critique of current practices in school counseling and counselor preparation. House and Sears then describe how counselor preparation programs must change if they are going to transform the practice of school counseling. Articles by Hanson and Stone, Hayes and Paisley, and Jackson et al. discuss innovative recruitment and selection strategies, how the curriculum must be restructured in training programs, and methods for improving the way counselors are inducted into their profession. Finally, articles by Musheno and Talbert and Hines portray how transformed school counselors will function in schools. To fully understand the changes needed in school counseling as well as the impact of the Transforming School Counseling Initiative, you are encouraged to read the articles in the order they are presented.

Susan Jones Sears
Guest Editor

References

Education Trust, The. (1999, May). *Dispelling the Myth: High Poverty Schools Exceeding Expectations*. Washington, DC: Author.

Patricia J. Martin

Transforming School Counseling: A National Perspective

EACH ONE OF US HAS THE RIGHT and responsibility to assess the roads that lie ahead and those roads of which we have traveled. And if the future road looms ominous and unpromising and the roads back uninviting, then we need to gather our resolve and carrying only the necessary baggage, step off that road to a new direction. (Angelou, 1993)

The mission for schools in the 21st century focuses squarely on effective teaching and learning. Standards-based education reform, with a relentless call for accountability and increased academic achievement for all students, comes at a time of booming technological advances and rapidly changing diversity in the composition of U.S. schools. The convergence of these forces, coupled with a critical look at school counseling at the close of the 20th century, provided a perfect opportunity for re-thinking, re-framing, and transforming the role of school counseling in American schools.

In 1996 the Education Trust, a Washington, DC-based nonprofit organization, with support from the DeWitt Wallace-Reader's Digest Fund, launched a five-year, multistaged national initiative for transforming school counseling. The Trust made public glaring points of disjunction in the theory being taught and the practice actually needed to help students, especially low-income and minority youth, improve academically in schools.

The findings of this initiative became the impetus for seeking and developing the fundamental changes needed to bring the work of school counselors into alignment with the mission of schools for the 21st century. Change for school counseling is not optional—it is mandatory for school counseling to survive in the rapidly changing environment of K-12 schools.

In this article, critical findings are shared about the status of school counseling in the nation, the gap between preparation and practice, and how the work of school counselors needs to connect to student achievement and education reform. It is these findings that were used to develop a framework for change in the field of school counseling.

Background Information

The Transforming School Counseling Initiative (TSCI) was implemented at the Education Trust with the express goal of encouraging the creation of new model programs for the pre-service training of school counselors. The purpose of these newly designed programs was to prepare graduates to serve as student advocates and academic advisors who demonstrate the belief that all students can achieve at high levels on rigorous, challenging academic course content. To launch this ambitious initiative, the Trust spent time in schools and communities across the country talking with school counselors, counselor educators, principals, teachers, parents, students, and other stakeholders.

Patricia J. Martin is the regional assistant vice president of The College Board Transforming School Counseling Initiative.

To accomplish the goal of developing new graduate-level school counseling preparation programs, the Education Trust set out to (a) assess the status of school counseling in the nation; (b) develop a plan for the reform of graduate-level preparation programs; (c) select six higher education institutions with K-12 school district partners to develop and implement new models for training school counselors; and (d) produce a plan for transforming the school counselor preparation programs in the nation.

The initiative purposefully concentrated on the actions of school counselors and the graduate-level preparation they received. The overarching purpose of the initiative was to open academic doors to all students, especially poor and minority students, so that these young people would be able to unconditionally participate in the complex technological economy of the 21st century.

Why focus on school counselors?

School counselors are in a critical position to focus on issues, strategies, and interventions that will assist in closing the achievement gap between low-income and minority students and their more advantaged peers. Low-income and minority students continue to leave school prior to graduation in alarming proportions, not because they are unable to succeed, but because they are underchallenged academically and are placed disproportionately in special education and low-level, remedial classes.

Low-income and minority students are most likely to be taught by the least skilled teachers. Their schools are also more likely to have fewer instructional resources, including up-to-date textbooks and laboratory equipment. In multiple ways, too many school administrators, teachers, and school counselors demonstrate by their actions that they hold low expectations for these students. Added to this conundrum is the fact that low-income and minority students often see no connection between what is being taught in school and a better future for themselves. The school counselor interventions needed to help these students connect school preparation with future career options is critical for the new millennium.

In some schools, despite often dire neighborhood conditions, low-income and minority students are succeeding at high levels. These are schools where all students are held to high academic standards, pushed to stretch and achieve, and given support throughout this process. In these schools there are significant adults who believe that low-income and minority students can succeed and who, through advocacy and action, create conditions to support this belief.

With a school-wide perspective, school counselors are in the best position to assess the school for systemic and other barriers that impede academic success for all students. Issues of equity, access, and supporting conditions for success come to rest at the counselor's desk in the form of data about student achievement, community conditions, and reports of school failure. Thus, school counselors who have served as record keepers of student data in schools are ideally positioned to use this data to advocate for traditionally underserved students. But most counselors are not prepared to provide such leadership.

The traditional mental health-focused training provided to school counselors over the past decades may have provided ample skill development for practitioners to help students with personal and social challenges, but it falls devastatingly short of helping students succeed academically in schools of the 21st century. Because of the recent accountability demands for all students to reach high academic standards, practicing school counselors must be prepared to function as advocates for high academic achievement. Not only must they heighten their role in providing for the academic and career domains of school counseling, but they must also be prepared to provide leadership for other professionals to join in this endeavor. School counselors have great influence over students' academic placements, and, thus, hold critical keys to students' career futures.

The National Perspective of School Counseling

In 1996, the Education Trust conducted an assessment of the state of school counseling across the nation. The Trust examined both graduate-level preparation programs and the work of K-12 practitioners and reported these critical findings:

State of graduate-level preparation
1. Considerable change in the field of school counseling was already being discussed in 1996. Graduate-level counselor preparation program faculty,

professional guidance and counseling organizations, school districts, individual schools, and school counselors were openly talking about and/or seeking some kind of change.
2. The direction for change in the field of school counseling was not clearly articulated; national professional counseling conferences were using "change" in their themes, but content sessions at those conferences were not about change. Ideas about change were not coming from the traditional areas of research or professional organizations in ways that created vision and direction for practitioners and counselor educators.
3. Change in graduate-level school counselor preparation was largely being viewed as the "adding on of courses"—usually courses with a mental health or personal/social focus.
4. Changes in graduate-level counseling programs were mostly externally driven by state or other counselor accreditation and/or credentialing agencies.
5. Most counselor educators have little or no ongoing involvement with K-12 institutions, except when arranging practica and intern experiences for trainees.
6. There are few obvious pathways present for creating and using an integrated model for training other school professionals (e.g., teachers, administrators, psychologists) alongside counselors so that they might learn to work together in creating fertile, supportive environments for student academic success. Teaming and collaborations among these professionals was not a part of formal pre-service training.
7. Graduate-level preparation programs provide insufficient opportunities for field practice of skills and knowledge.
8. Many universities/colleges provide a large block of "generic counseling" courses as the core learning for all types of counselors; school counselors take these courses with community counselors, rehabilitation counselors, marriage and family counselors, etc. These courses often make little or no connections to school, learning, children, adolescents, and youth.
9. Facilitating student learning, improving student achievement, creating access and support for all students to rigorous academic preparation are issues not seen as a primary emphasis for school counselors. These issues receive little or no emphasis in graduate-level preparation of school counselors, but they are the primary focus of schooling, education reform, and the accountability measures in today's climate.
10. It is the exception, rather than the rule, that data are systematically collected, reviewed, and used in program change and renewal by practicing counselors and counselor educators.
11. School counselor education programs are staffed with large numbers of professional psychologists without school counseling experience or training. Often the educators with school experience are adjunct staff members with full-time jobs in school settings. Their impact on the philosophy, focus, and change in programs is limited.
12. In higher education, there are incentives and rewards for counselor educators to become specialists in a specific area—the suicide expert, the multicultural expert, the group counseling expert, the gang expert, etc. This situation leads to "silo teaching" where much energy is given to specific topics by individual staff members with little or no integration across topics or collective focus on developing, implementing, and sustaining a total program philosophy.
13. Counselor training programs providing early and frequent practice along with theory were considered by practitioners to be the best models for preparation for working in schools.
14. Understanding how to be an effective counselor in a school setting—maximizing the acquired skills and knowledge received in training—should be part of the pre-service program for school counseling.
15. Use of technology is noticeably absent from counselor preparation programs.
16. Collaboration between K-12 school districts and institutions of higher education holds the best possible chance for authentic program transformation, including change in field practice.

State of K-12 school counseling
1. Large numbers of practicing school counselors are functioning as highly paid clerical staff, quasi administrators and/or inadequately trained therapeutic mental health providers with unmanageable client loads. Their role/function is sometimes dictated by the district, the principal, the community in which they work, and/or their own personal preference.
2. Many school counselors believe they have the best jobs in the world. Some of them wouldn't change a thing about what they do where they are. They have found their niche in life—and they want to hold on to it. Everything is fine as it is! They love their students, role, work setting, and all that that means.
3. Some see the job of school counselor as a promotion from the classroom, a kind of bonus—limited student contact and freedom from the classroom responsibilities of a teacher.
4. Some counselors see themselves as "saviors"—save the children from whatever might "hurt them." Sadly, the "whatever" sometimes includes saving them from principals, teachers, parents, and others who

believe that students should be challenged to do more, achieve more, and stretch in order to master rigorous course content.

5. Some counselors in K-12 schools would like to reduce their client loads, operating on the belief that they could really get more done with students if only they had more counselors in the building.

6. Some of them would like a change of schools, change of principals, change of students they serve (i.e., "If only I had better students, more materials, a bigger office, more understanding teachers, a stronger, more child-oriented principal, superintendent, or board of education. If only the students were like they used to be! If only we had better children, better schools, better parents. If only there were no poverty, drugs, gangs, violence, etc.").

7. Some school counselors—as is true in any profession—are nearing retirement and have developed apathy and a lack of interest in the futures of the students they may not be around to see graduate.

8. Many school counselors are just entering the profession, are excited about their work, and are ready and able to take their place as an educator and counselor that will leave the world a better place. They are looking for ways to make what they do more meaningful for their students and the communities they serve.

9. Some counselors are into their mid-life crisis. They arrive at work daily and ask: What is a person like me doing in a place like this? Should I be retraining to do something different? Am I effective at what I do? When will I ever be appreciated for all the hard work I do and am doing daily? Do my principal, students, parents, and teachers even know what I do? Do they even care?

What does all of this mean?

Even though, when taken together, these findings were distressing, none of the information found by the Trust was new. To the contrary, earlier focus groups conducted across the nation readily provided the Trust with concrete examples and evidence validating the information. What the Trust did find, however, was an opportunity to look critically at school counseling practiced in the venue of schools—a place where school success was defined as all students reaching measurable high academic standards. The Trust also had the opportunity to capture the best practices in both higher education institutions and K-12 districts, those practices that resulted in student benefits that supported schools in their efforts to raise academic achievement for all children. Contextualizing school counseling practice in the reality and demands of standards-based education reform required that both higher education institutions and K-12 school districts be part of any solutions for change. Additionally, promising practices occurring in both K-12 school districts and institutions of higher education were important in constructing a vision and a plan for transforming school counseling.

It's been said that if you don't know where you're going, any road will get you there. Knowing one's destination, however, requires more thoughtful attention to the paths taken, and provides the traveler with indisputable knowledge of having arrived at the desired destination. The TSCI started with the end in mind: changing the preparation of school counselors in the U.S. The destination became putting school counselors squarely in the middle of K-12 education reform as integral players whose express goal is to remove barriers that impede academic success for all students, and to do so in ways that would not exclude poor and minority students. Once the destination was established, institutions and stakeholders involved in the transformation mapped ways to identify the skills and knowledge needed to get there.

What would change mean?

The roads school counselors and counselor educators have traveled and are traveling, as well as those of all educators in the 21st century, are under critical review. Measurable performance in terms of increased academic achievement for all students is the driving force of education reform. Professionals who do not add to this bottom line are considered superfluous to schools. Making school counselors integral players in education reform required a new vision, new ways of looking at "helping." Two of the three counseling domains—academic and career—approved by the American School Counselor Association (ASCA) had to assume more prominent positions in school counseling programs. And, school counselors' efforts to "help" students in these areas had to be tied to the mission of schools to produce measurable increases in student achievement. With a healthy amount of consternation, professional school counselors and counselor educators took on the task of gathering the resolve needed to step off the roads they knew, and in which they felt a great degree of comfort, to a new direction.

A New Direction for School Counseling

The new vision for school counseling was designed to:

1. Move school counseling from a position of comfort or maintaining the status quo to one of cutting-edge social action, advocacy for access, and support for success for all students, especially those that have not been served well in the past.
2. Move school counseling from an ancillary service-oriented profession to one that becomes a critical player in accomplishing the mission of schools, academic success and high achievement for all students.
3. Move school counseling from the position of making students feel good or providing mental health services to one of aggressively empowering young people to construct successful futures. Counselors must help students obtain the academic preparation needed to ensure they have substantial postsecondary options, and, thus, better futures in a global technological world.
4. Move school counseling from a profession that states that it believes in the worth of all human beings to one that can document and measure deliberate behaviors, interactions, and concrete results in a school setting that solidly affirm this belief.

Stepping off well-traveled roads to embrace new possibilities takes courage and a willingness to take risks. Like other pioneers who dare to challenge the limits of existing frontiers, practitioners and counselor educators seeking to institute new practices and training are not always met with open arms by their peers.

As a result of the findings from the first stage of the TSCI, the Trust formed an advisory board of critical stakeholders who worked for a period of 14 months developing a new vision for school counseling, identifying the scope of the work, and constructing the eight essential elements that needed to change if school counseling is to survive. House and Sears (this issue) will focus on these eight elements of change in their article.

What will school counselors have to know and be able to do?

1. Focus on improving student achievement. Forget the deficit model and quit trying to fix a few kids while not having time for the many.
2. Help children learn, help their teachers motivate them, and help parents successfully navigate the school bureaucracy so that they, too, can advocate for their children.
3. Understand and use social advocacy skills to challenge the status quo in schools and systems where inequities impede students' access to quality academic preparation.
4. Use data to affect change and advocate for those students who need help in navigating school bureaucracies to get access to rigorous courses and quality teaching.
5. Understand organizational change and how to intervene to make change happen for children.
6. Become competent users of technology to monitor individual students' progress, and help students and their families gather information needed for critical decisions about their children's future options and plans.
7. Use their group and problem-solving skills with other educational professionals for the purpose of systemic problem solving.
8. Understand and be able to operate competently in a diverse multicultural school setting and community.

How school counselors-in-training gain the knowledge and skills listed above is another story. In 1997, the Education Trust selected six university/school district partnerships to develop and implement model programs to transform school counseling. The six institutions and their K-12 school district partners are:

- California State University-Northridge and a portion of L.A. Unified Schools
- Indiana State University and Vigo County Corporation
- The Ohio State University and the Columbus Public Schools
- State University of West Georgia and Clayton County Public Schools
- The University of Georgia and Athens-Clarke Public Schools
- University of North Florida and the Duval County Public Schools

The six universities and the partner districts have resolved to chart a new direction for school counseling. Several articles included in this issue on school counseling will describe how the six universities have transformed their preparation programs to ensure that their trainees will graduate with the skills needed to transform the work of school counselors.

Conclusion

This article has provided a critical look at school counseling and at the way universities prepare counselors. Findings from a national initiative led by the Education Trust point to the need for change both in the preparation of school counselors and in the way school districts use their skills once they are hired. Finally, the author suggests ways counselor training programs should change and proposes the knowledge and skills counselors need if they are going to survive in the 21st century.

References

Angelou, M. (1993). *Wouldn't take nothing for my journey now.* New York: Random House.

Education Trust, The. (1997, February). *The national guidance and counseling reform program.* Washington, DC: Author.

Reese M. House
Susan Jones Sears

Preparing School Counselors to be Leaders and Advocates: A Critical Need in the New Millennium

IN THIS ARTICLE WE PROPOSE a new approach to the preparation of school counselors as a means of preparing them to work in 21st-century schools. It is critical that school counselors move beyond their current roles as helper-responders in order to become proactive leaders and advocates for the success of all students. We believe that when school counselors are taught to question the beliefs, assumptions, and values behind inequitable school policies, structures, or actions they become an integral part of schools and educational reform. This process of learning how to examine and question the inequitable practices that some students experience needs to start in counselor preparation programs. This can be done by emphasizing the value of experience, promoting active learning, engaging in reflective practice, and inviting dialogue among students and faculty. Such themes can guide program development, classroom exchanges, field experiences, interactions with colleagues, and collaboration with community members. Through these processes, school counselors are taught to take stands against injustices and join counselor educators and community stakeholders in thoughtfully constructing a blueprint for student academic success.

Reese M. House is a program specialist at The Education Trust Transforming School Counseling Initiative; Susan Jones Sears is associate professor of education at The Ohio State University.

We describe how counselor educators can prepare school counselors to become action-oriented, critical thinkers. We also encourage the creation of learning communities among counselors-in-training and the schools, students, families, and communities they will ultimately serve. We hope students who internalize and use the skills gained from this teaching will become professionals who embrace change, continually reflect on practice, and constantly seek to serve all students.

Rationale for Changes in School Counseling

Throughout the United States, communities are striving to improve their schools. To date, major school reform efforts have focused on accountability for student performance by setting more rigorous academic standards, building new assessment strategies, and restructuring preservice and in-service experiences for teachers and administrators (Mohrman & Lawler, 1996). In the United States, two primary events have fueled these efforts: (a) the unrelenting call for accountability for educating all students to higher academic standards, and (b) the economic demand for a more knowledgeable workforce. Concurrent with demands for accountability, reform is driven by the awareness that the student population has become more diverse and now includes increased numbers of poor and minority children living in urban and rural communities.

Data from states and local school districts show that poor students and students of color are systemically denied an education that leads them to success in school and in the marketplace (Achievement in America, 2000). This data points out a significant achievement gap between poor and minority students and their more advantaged peers (Haycock, 1998).

Current Forces Shaping School Counseling

Why don't most school counselors involve themselves in educational reform efforts and actively work to promote academic success for all students? The answer to this question is complex. Current school counselor behavior results from inadequate preservice training, conflicting roles, administrators who fail to utilize counselors' skills, pliable and overly accommodating counselor behavior, limited professional development opportunities, and overt and covert pressures from school, community, and parental special interest groups (Walz, 1997).

Most importantly, when school counselors lack a strong personal/professional compass, their own well-conceived vision or mission, defined programs, and identified role, they function at the direction of others. School administrators, parents with special interests, teachers, and others often insist on the adoption of their agendas for school counselors (American School Counselor Association [ASCA], 1998). Counselors comply too often.

Unfortunately, this means that school counselors often serve as maintainers of the status quo, advocating for the school system rather than for students and marginalized groups. They become "sorters and selectors," perpetuating the accepted placements and systemic barriers that cause an inequitable distribution between achievers and nonachievers based on race and socio-economic status (Hart & Jacobi, 1992).

School counselor preparation programs: Current status

Martin (this issue) describes the deficiencies in counselor preparation programs. Traditional counselor education programs, for the most part, have not provided learning opportunities that prepare school counselors to be knowledgeable about education reform issues, or how to be vital players in implementing reform strategies in schools. School counselors have not been taught about social and systems change, political climates, and power structures of schools and communities. They have not been taught elements of leadership and collaboration that would enable them to effectively instigate or facilitate systemic change. Counselor educators have not designed their curricula to teach advocacy, question the status quo, and challenge systems (Capuzzi, 1998; Education Trust, 1997).

Systems Change

Education systems can either discourage or empower students to critically question systemic inconsistencies (Darder, 1991). Educational systems that discourage students perpetuate the creation of obedient, moldable, passive, and low-paid future workers incapable of changing systems. On the other hand, educational systems that empower students educate them to become critical involved citizens (McLaren, 1989). In our proposal to change school counseling, we assume that counselors can make a difference in promoting academic success if they first develop a broad social consciousness and a critical awareness of conditions in society and schools that impinge on that success (Southers, 1991).

When counselor educators promote systemic change through critical inquiry, they empower counselors to be leaders and change agents in society (Darling-Hammond, 1993). From this perspective, counseling professionals need to influence the social, cultural, and political dynamics that undergird academic success. Advocating for high achievement for all students is proposed here as a key role for counselors. It places them at the center of the mission of schooling and educational reform.

Motivating and preparing for action

What will prompt counselor educators to change? First, counselor educators themselves must believe that change is necessary. Second, they must be convinced that these changes will benefit the counselor education students, the students in K-12 schools, and the community at large. Then, the question becomes, "Is it possible to design such a system-challenging, visionary curriculum from within institutions that do not necessarily reward such change?" We recommend that counselor educators begin by critically examining their own beliefs.

Examining beliefs. Counselor educators may want to begin examining what they believe by asking themselves these fundamental questions:

1. What do I believe about my own ability to be a leader and a change agent?
2. What are the current gaps between preparation and practice in K-12 schools?
3. How do the graduates of my program demonstrate accountability for their work?
4. What do I believe about the ability of all school-aged students to reach high academic standards?
5. How does my behavior as an instructor impact the students I teach?

Examining the need for change. Reflective inquiry about current program practices may help counselor educators decide the depth and breadth of changes that may be necessary. The following questions may stimulate discussion:

1. Are we currently preparing school counselors to work effectively in schools?
2. How might we respond more actively in changing curricula to meet the current needs of school counseling students?
3. What might we do differently in influencing the structure of our school counseling programs?
4. How can we create a cohesive school counseling curricula that is closely aligned with the mission of schools and schooling?
5. How would working actively in a learning community enhance my teaching?
6. What do we believe school counselors need to know and be able to do?
7. How do we change our current teaching methods to be responsive to the feedback we have received from counselors we have taught?
8. How do we use data on schools and student achievement to make changes in our program?
9. How do we teach others to think systemically about schools, learning, and achievement?
10. As instructors, how do we model leadership, advocacy, and systemic change?

Examining how systems change. After examining their personal beliefs and what steps might be necessary for change, counselor educators can look at the systems that need to change. Key elements in a system include the internal university environment (department chair, dean, provost), the near external environment (local area schools, community, business), and the more remote external environment (state legislature, board of education, certification bodies). These entities all assist or deter change. Counselor educators may want to ask themselves the following:

1. What are the beliefs, assumptions, and values behind a particular policy, structure, action, or orientation? Who shares these beliefs?
2. What are the historical sources of these beliefs?
3. Whose knowledge is considered legitimate?
4. Who prospers if we act according to the identified beliefs?
5. Who is empowered, disempowered, or disenfranchised by these beliefs?

The answers to these questions may offer insight into the feasibility of making changes in school counselor preparation.

Action questions. Those ready to move toward implementation of a new approach to counselor preparation can ask the following questions to guide them in taking further steps:

1. What is necessary to develop and nurture a community of learners in the classroom?
2. How do we define ourselves as a learning community?
3. How do we encourage dialogue that leads to generative solution finding rather than presenting ourselves as having most of the answers?
4. How do we decide what will be included or excluded from discussion or practice?
5. What kind of pedagogy, experiences, and modeling best prepare critical, reflective practitioners?
6. How do we encourage a diversity of views and alternatives?
7. How do we call attention to social injustices and inequities?
8. How have we helped students develop and exercise their voices?

Goals for School Counselor Preparation

After counselor education faculty have engaged in such reflective soul searching, they then need to decide what changes to pursue. We suggest that counselor educators "begin with the end in mind" (Covey, 1992, p. 42) and look at the product of counselor education; that is, what school counselors themselves would do if they worked as leaders and advocates for change in the schools. In addition to being skilled counselors who work with students' personal concerns, school counselors should

1. Behave as if they expect all students to achieve at a high level.
2. Actively work to remove barriers to learning.
3. Teach students how to help themselves (e.g., organization, study, and test-taking skills).
4. Teach students and their families how to successfully manage the bureaucracy of the school system; for example, teach parents how to (a) enroll their children in academic courses that will lead to college, (b) make formal requests to school officials on various matters, and (c) monitor the academic progress of their children.
5. Teach students and their families how to access support systems that encourage academic success by (a) informing students and parents about tutoring and academic enrichment opportunities, and (b) teaching students and parents how to find resources on preparation for standardized tests.
6. Use local, regional, and national data on disparities in resources and academic achievement to promote system change.
7. Work collaboratively with all school personnel.
8. Organize community activities to promote supportive structures for high standards for all students (e.g., after-school tutoring programs at neighborhood religious settings).
9. Help parents and communities organize efforts to work with schools to institute and support high standards for all children.

Widening the lens of what school counselors see as their job implies the formation of a new training model, one based in systems thinking about schools and schooling.

Necessary Programmatic Changes

We propose a mission-driven model and a set of guidelines—eight essential elements for change—to revise school counselor preparation curriculum. These eight elements reflect the work of the Education Trust Advisory Committee (Martin, this issue). The eight essential elements that counselor education programs must address if they are to successfully transform their preparation programs include (a) criteria for selection and recruitment of candidates for counselor preparation programs; (b) curricular content, structure, and sequence of courses; (c) methods of instruction, field experiences, and practice; (d) induction process into the profession; (e) working relationships with community partners; (f) professional development for counselor educators; (g) university/school district partnerships; and (h) university/state department of education partnerships. Counselor education faculty can use these elements as a framework for organizing, planning, and implementing program changes.

Developing a mission-driven program

An overriding principle of any counselor education program, and a prerequisite to using the eight essential elements as an organizational model, is the development of a mission statement. A clear mission statement for school counselor preparation becomes the driving force of the program. It helps shape the curriculum as well as the practicing counselors who graduate from the program. We recommend an inclusive mission-creating process. Including nonuniversity community partners in developing a mission statement, results in greater relevance to the needs of counselors, administrators, teachers, and students in schools. To develop a mission statement, school counselor educators can begin by looking at what they believe and value about (a) educational attainment for all students; (b) future career options for students they serve; (c) what school counselors should know and be able to do when they complete the program; and (d) measurable outcomes for the work of school counselors.

For example, the faculty at California State University at Northridge developed a mission statement that reflects a new approach to school counselor preparation. This mission statement evolved during eight months of collaboration among parents, school counselors, school administrators, community representatives, and faculty in both counselor and teacher education. Here is the resulting statement:

> The CSUN School Counseling and Guidance Program, in the Department of Educational Psychology and Counseling, is a multi-disciplinary team effort designed to ensure that participating students reach high academic performance and professional competence to plan, organize, and implement comprehensive, results-based school guidance programs that affect high academic achievement and preparation for success in a 4-year college or university among pre-K through 12th grade public school students. (Hanson & Geary, 2000)

Eight essential elements for change

1. Criteria for selection and recruitment of candidates for counselor preparation. Typically, counselor education programs have not actively recruited students to their programs; instead, they have either accepted all applicants or used a screening process to select an identified number of students each year. Program faculty often state that a graduate school that requires certain scores on GRE qualifying examinations hamstrings them.

Rather than following the "standard" procedures already in place, faculty can develop new criteria for selection based on the mission of the program. This means questioning the current systemic regulations that prevent candidates from diverse backgrounds from enrolling in the program. Because of the increasing number of students of color in U.S. schools, it is critical that school counselors represent diverse ethnic backgrounds.

Instituting this "Active Admissions" process becomes a way for counselor educators to model leadership and advocacy for other faculty. First steps include questioning all current procedures to see if they are serving the desired purposes, and gaining the number of qualified students wanted in the program. After a review of current procedures, implementation strategies might include such approaches as (a) working with local school districts to identify teachers that might be excellent counselors; (b) devising a nomination process so community and school members can nominate prospective students; (c) creating an active recruiting committee consisting of faculty, practicing school counselors, students, community members, and school administrators; (d) making recruiting visits to historically Black and Hispanic institutions; and (e) working with the campus equity center to recruit candidates.

In addition to these recruitment processes, it will be necessary to revisit the selection procedures. Who is involved in the selection process? On what basis are students admitted to the program? What questions are asked of applicants? How are applicants screened? Are group or individual interviews conducted? This may be an excellent opportunity to include school and community members by inviting them to participate in the selection process. Thus, they become more invested in counselors working in schools.

After a review of the selection, recruitment, and admissions processes, the new process is made public. The mission statement, which includes the intent of the program, should be included in the admissions materials. One by-product of this new process is that students will self-select from the program. If they are not seeking training to be advocates, leaders, and change agents, but rather want to be "helpers" and start a clinical practice, then this may not be the program for them. On the other hand, word will spread about the kind of preparation in your program, and the new admissions standards will attract more "qualified" candidates.

2. Curricular content, structure, and sequence of courses. Once the mission of the program has been clarified, it directs the content, structure, and sequencing of courses. Some questions to consider: What course content, skills, and knowledge are essential to producing school counselors to meet the program mission statement? What is the rationale for the sequence of courses in the program? How does the program integrate the philosophy/mission into the teaching, curriculum, and course sequence? How does the mission influence pedagogy? How will you collaborate with other important stakeholders in the development of the new curricula content, structure, and sequence of courses?

Some innovations that might be considered are delivering coursework creatively and developing learning communities.

Counselor educators need to consider alternative means of course delivery, such as (a) teaching at public schools or in the community; (b) inviting school counselors and administrators to co-teach some classes; (c) scheduling more courses on weekends; (d) offering more courses through distance education; or (e) teaming with faculty from educational administration to co-teach a course for both administrators and counselors. By diversifying the location and/or delivery of instruction, there is a shift away from the concept of the university as the seat of knowledge. This broadens the universe from which knowledge is gained. The University of Wisconsin at Milwaukee designed one successful example of an alternative delivery method, in cooperation with the Milwaukee Public Schools. They admitted teachers from a large school district and worked collaboratively with district personnel to co-teach these students in a cohort model. A majority of the classes were taught in the public schools at times convenient to teachers.

Strong learning communities can provide modeling, reflection opportunities, and group interaction for school counseling students (Ward & House, 1998). A learning community emphasizes inquiry and supports different social and cultural contexts. In the learning community, knowledge is challenged, redefined, and negotiated by all participants (Griffen, 1993). It is our premise that this approach allows future school counselors to gain insights into the social and cultural implications of different ways of knowing, different forms of knowledge, and different approaches to research.

One way to encourage the development of a learning community in the counselor education program is to utilize a cohort model of training (Paisley & Hayes, 2000). In a cohort model, a group of students enters and progresses through the program together. Also, instructors plan activities in courses, practica, and internships that require students to regularly work collaboratively. Use of a cohort model creates the expectations among students that they ought to collaborate with others, and provides a model that is usable later as school counselors. Osborne et al. (1998) elaborated on the use of a cohort model and emphasized the benefits of a cohort model coupled with a retreat experience designed to build cohesiveness.

In cohort models, individuals examine interpersonal dynamics and learn to value the unique worldview of each participant. Communication, negotiation, and conflict management become vehicles for enhanced learning. Cohort models use teaming, peer coaching, generative problem solving, and collaboration, methods that are critical to school counselors becoming leaders and advocates in their schools and communities.

3. Methods of instruction, field experiences, and practice. In this new approach to teaching school counselors, the methods of instruction, field experiences, and practica would be transformed to include (a) early experiential learning in the schools; (b) early and continuous integration of theory and practice; and (c) frequent opportunities for counselors to know and understand schools and schooling. The program faculty would focus on (a) learning rather than teaching; (b) induction-oriented, interactive teaching rather than lecture; (c) sharing belief systems; (d) modeling advocacy, leadership, and community involvement; (e) collaborating and teaming with school and community stakeholders; (f) modeling the use of data to make informed decisions for systemic change; and (g) placing students in the school system early and frequently.

Counselor educators' ongoing experience in schools models for students an investment in collaborative work. The vast differences between how counselors are often taught and how they actually work in the schools may be reduced by building such collaborative relationships with school district administrators, supervisors, teachers, and counselors. Early, frequent, and direct experience in the schools exposes future counselors and university faculty to the daily lives of students, families, teachers, counselors, administrators, schools, and the community. In this process they learn counseling models, child and family counseling approaches, social service case-management approaches, community resources, and systemic paradigms of change. In addition, they become familiar with education reform issues, gain knowledge of the achievement gap, learn how to collect and use data, and develop an understanding of standards-based assessment, testing and interpretation, special education, and school policy.

Reflectivity, as it applies to schooling, is a conscious effort by school counselors to identify contradictions and hidden or distorted understandings existent in the schools (Lather, 1986). Learning to practice reflectivity helps future counselors to "think outside of the box" and question the status quo.

Such a reflective inquiry method can highlight the social and political patterns preventing access and equity to a quality education for all students in public schools. In this reflective mode, counselor educators are asked to contemplate fundamental questions about what they do, how they do it, and what it means both for themselves as professionals and those they teach. Reflective practice includes recognizing professional dilemmas and inconsistencies, using them to construct meaning, and from such meaning, developing guides for action (Colton & Sparks-Langer, 1993; Mezirow, 1994).

Strategies that counselor educators could employ in their classes to teach reflectivity include the following:

1. *Reflective journaling.* Writing out confusions, frustrations, questions, intentions, hypotheses, and assumptions pertaining to students or classroom events.
2. *Retrospection.* Drawing together materials (case notes, reflective pad, or literature) that link practice to the articulation of those values, beliefs, and concepts.
3. *Reflective supervision.* Reviewing during supervision the purpose, beliefs, and assumptions of school counseling to aid in clarifying patterns and themes necessary for learning and professional growth.
4. *Reflective dialogue.* Reviewing journal entries and other reflections with peers, focusing on what happened, what is being learned, and the meaning of the events; extending this reflective dialogue beyond peers to school and community members to widen and enrich the learning.
5. *Action research.* Reviewing the literature, applying the relevant findings to counseling in schools, conducting an action research study, and reflecting on this research process.

It is important to note that in this process of teaching students to be reflective they will begin to challenge, question, and push the envelope on a variety of issues with the instructors. This becomes an opportunity to dialogue with students about advocacy, leadership, and change. This is not a passive exercise, but an active, involved, and engaged process in which open dialogue and exchange of ideas are encouraged and supported. The classroom becomes a safe place for introducing new ideas and new ways of looking at systems change, and prepares students for such exchanges in schools. This is a very different way of teaching than a lecture or planned discussion on selected topics.

4. Induction process into the profession. Preparation to be a school counselor starts when students apply for the program. Program faculty need to identify how induction into the profession is included both as part of the preparation program, and after completion of the program. Often the most difficult part of becoming a school counselor is putting into practice in the schools the skills and knowledge learned in the program. Developing and maintaining professional relationships and making a difference in the profession become critical roles for the new school counselor. For school counselors to work as questioners of the status quo and initiators of action, they need continuing support, constant reflectivity and feedback, and a period of mentoring by practicing counselors and counselor educators. The following questions should be considered by counselor educators during the new counselor induction phase:

1. What critical experiences and professional involvement are needed during the preparation program?
2. What kind of follow-up support (e.g., mentors) does the faculty provide for new school counselors?
3. How does the faculty contribute to continuing professional development activities for school counselors that support the program philosophy, mission, and goals?
4. How does the faculty encourage and support new school counselors to take risks for youth, including those that challenge the system?
5. How does the program assist new school counselors to obtain allies who might support them in their work?

5. Developing working relationships with community partners. One of the tenets of the education reform movement is the belief that schools cannot function successfully without supportive community partnerships (Gerstner, Semerad, Doyle, & Johnston, 1994; Schorr, 1997). The creation of successful school counselor training programs also depends on strong and viable community partnerships. The essential nature of this endeavor is based in the concept that change agents receive ultimate direction from the community (Homan, 1999).

> You are working with a community rather than having a community working with you. The change agent must listen to the community as well as offer direction. It is the community who must act, not just the change agent, and the final decisions will always reside with the community. After all, whose change is it anyway?" (p. 10)

As counselor educators consider working with community partners to gain insight and information, they might consider questions such as, What is the relationship between the community, local schools, and the counselor preparation program? How do we engage critical stakeholders in meaningful dialogue about training school counselors? What collaborative efforts exist to support closing the achievement gap among students of different socioeconomic classes and races?

6. Increasing professional development relevant to school counseling. Counselor educators need to choose professional development activities that increase their knowledge of schools. They may need to consider such questions as, What professional development activities will help me to prepare school counselors in a new model? How am I engaged in focused, reflective discussion on the current changes in philosophy, program, and role of school counselors? For example, many counselor educators teaching in school counselor preparation programs have either not worked in schools, or not worked in schools in a long time. Counselor educators can begin their professional development by becoming directly involved in the schools (Hayes, Dagley, & Horne, 1996). Such involvement helps educators better understand current education reform issues as well as current mandated accountability measures.

7. University/school district partnerships. Close and continuous collaboration with school districts is an essential ingredient in this new process of preparing school counselors. Best practices happen at both the university and in K-12 schools. Neither higher education nor school districts can design and implement the significant changes needed for school counselors independently. While school counselors and administrators are anchored in the reality of schools, students, and learning, counselor educators are steeped in research and theory. Working as collaborative stakeholders to create this new curriculum, including field experiences, ultimately ends in greater acceptance of the new directions. Together, a cohesive, reality-based, research-guided curricula can be designed and implemented.

8. University/state department of education partnerships. Influencing policy at the state level becomes an integral part of success in this new model. State department entities determine policy and thus program directions. However, there is often no clear working relationship or open lines of communication among state departments, universities, and school districts. It is important to become a part of the process and influence changes made at the state level regarding such policies as testing, certification, accreditation, and licensing. State departments of education and legislatures affect counselor training as much as national accreditation standards do.

Groups that have a wide base of community, school, and university representation have the best chance to influence state departments. Therefore, using a collaborative stakeholder group to identify, formulate, and convey directions the state might take enhances the chances for change. This collaborative group must develop a united and focused approach based in the interest of serving all children. A thoughtful and planned approach, utilizing data and including key stakeholders, will often make the difference in policy changes.

Conclusion

As leaders and advocates, counselor educators and school counselors need to reexamine recurrent professional role patterns and think in a more systemic fashion. They must reach and influence people beyond their jurisdiction, have political skills to cope with conflicting requirements of multiple constituencies, and question the status quo. When working from this framework, counseling professionals will be active creators and definers of system changes and not passive respondents or victims of environmental circumstance. Preparation that produces school counselors who can practice as leaders and advocates to influence the attainment of high achievement for all students, aligns school counselors with educational reform, and places them in the middle of the changes needed to support all students.

In this article we have purposely looked beyond the usual boundaries and faculty roles of the university as we propose changes in school counselor preparation. We suggest anchoring learning in the experience of the schools and communities by forming collaborative working relationships with key stakeholders in school districts and communities.

We propose that counselor educators teach school counselors to be advocates, leaders, helpers, collaborators, risk-takers, and data-users. To do this, counselor educators need to both teach and model these roles themselves. We hope the questions presented in this article will guide counselor educators to (a) reflect on their practice, (b) participate in a planned dialogue with colleagues and others, (c) infuse new principles in their teaching of school counselors, and (d) become social activists in their roles as counselor educators. By doing this they will influence a new generation of school counselors to become leaders and advocates in the schools.

References

American School Counselor Association. (1998). *The national standards for school counseling programs.* Alexandria, VA: Author.

Capuzzi, D. (1998). Addressing the needs of at-risk youth: Early prevention and systemic intervention. In C.C. Lee & G.R. Walz (Eds.), *Social action: A mandate for counselors* (pp. 99-116). Alexandria, VA: American Counseling Association.

Colton, A.B., & Sparks-Langer, G.M. (1993). A conceptual framework to guide the development of teacher reflection and decision-making. *Journal of Teacher Education, 44,* 45-54.

Covey, S.R. (1992). *Principle-centered leadership.* New York: Fireside.

Darder, A. (1991). *Culture and power in the classroom: A critical foundation for bicultural education.* New York: Bergin & Gravey Press.

Darling-Hammond, L. (1993). Reframing the school reform agenda. *Phi Delta Kappan, 74*(10), 752-761.

Education Trust, The. (1997, February). *The national guidance and counseling reform program.* Washington, DC: Author.

Education Trust. (2000). *Achievement in America: 2000* [Computer diskette]. Washington DC: Author.

Gerstner, L.V., Semerad, R.D., Doyle, D.P., & Johnston, W.B. (1994). *Reinventing education: Entrepreneurship in America's public schools.* New York: Penguin Books.

Griffen, B. (1993). ACES: Promoting professionalism, collaboration, and advocacy. *Counselor Education and Supervision, 33,* 2-9.

Hanson, C., & Geary, P. (2000, March). *Mission driven programs: New directions for school counselors.* Paper presented at the annual meeting of the American Counseling Association, Washington, DC.

Hart, P.J., & Jacobi, M. (1992). *From gatekeeper to advocate: Transforming the role of the school counselor.* New York: College Entrance Examination Board.

Haycock, K. (1998). Good teaching matters: How well-qualified teachers can close the gap. *Thinking K-16, 3*(2), 1-2.

Hayes, R.L., Dagley, J., & Horne, A.M. (1996). Restructuring school counselor education: Work in progress. *Journal of Counseling & Development, 74,* 378-384.

Homan, M.S. (1999). *Rules of the game: Lessons from the field of community change.* Pacific Grove, CA: Brooks/Cole.

Lather, P. (1986). Research as praxis. *Harvard Educational Review, 56*(3), 257-277.

McLaren, P. (1989). *Life in schools: An introduction to critical pedagogy in the foundations of education.* New York: Longman.

Mezirow, J. (1994). Understanding transformation theory. *Adult Education Quarterly 44*(4), 222-244.

Mohrman, S.A., & Lawler, E.E. (1996). Motivation for school reform. In S.H. Fuhrman & J.A. O'Day (Eds.), *Rewards and reform: Creating educational incentives that work* (pp. 115-143). San Francisco: Jossey-Bass.

Osborne, J.L., Collison, B.B., House, R.M., Gray, L.A., Firth, J., & Lou, M. (1998). Developing a social advocacy model for counselor education. *Counselor Education & Supervision, 37,* 190-202.

Paisley, P.O., & Hayes, R.L. (2000). Counselor under construction: Implications for program design. In G. McAuliffe & K. Eriksen (Eds.), *Preparing counselors and therapists: Creating constructivist and developmental programs.* Alexandria, VA: ACES and Donning Publishers.

Schorr, L.B. (1997). *Common purpose: Strengthening families and neighborhoods to rebuild America.* New York: Anchor Books.

Southers, C.L. (1991). Home economics teacher education reform: Prime time for a phoenix agenda. *Journal of Vocational Home Economics Education, 9*(2), 56-69.

Walz, G.R. (1997). *Knowledge generalizations regarding the status of guidance and counseling.* Washington, DC: The Education Trust.

Ward, C.C., & House, R.M. (1998). Counseling supervision: A reflective model. *Counselor Education and Supervision, 38,* 23-33.

Charles Hanson
Carolyn Stone

Recruiting Leaders to Transform School Counseling

THE UNITED STATES IS GROWING rapidly into a more diverse nation, increasing the demand for a diverse workforce of educators. However, the lack of diversity and availability of educators is reaching crisis proportion (Orfield & Yun, 1999). This lack of diversity is especially evident among school counselors. While the K-12 student population in today's public schools has a large representation of minority racial and ethnic groups, the majority of school counselors are White (D'Andrea & Arredondo, 1999; Lee, 1995). This underrepresentation of minorities is also reflected in counselor education faculty, department chairpersons, and students in graduate programs (Brotherton, 1996; Young, Chamley, & Withers, 1990). Eighty-three percent of students in nationally accredited counseling graduate programs identify themselves as "White" (Dinsmore & England, 1996). "This sort of institutional arrangement reflects a type of racial . . . domination that, at the very least, unwittingly perpetuates cultural encapsulation within the profession" (Brotherton, 1996, p. 5).

A student today can go through 12 years of education without ever having a teacher, administrator, or school counselor who is a member of an ethnic minority (National Center for Educational Statistics, 1997). While minority students in schools prefer counselors of their same race, ethnicity, and cultural background (Herring, 1997), very few are available to them. This may contribute to the finding that minority and low-income students receive fewer counseling services (Hart & Jacobi, 1992).

The search for and selection of minority candidates in school counseling programs is also critical to counselors' development of multicultural competence. Researchers in the field contend that such competence can only be gained through the mutual learning and interaction of diverse ethnic and cultural groups. "The courage to change and work cross-culturally is an active, interactive process. Individuals cannot learn about others in the abstract. When it comes to cultural differences, only reality counts" (Arredondo, 1999, p. 102). The importance of diversity and multicultural competence is further affirmed by professional associations and accrediting bodies (Arredondo et al., 1996; Council for Accreditation of Counseling and Related Educational Programs, 1994; Sue, Arredondo, & McDavis, 1992). Effective training in multicultural competence requires school counseling programs to increase the diversity in their student groups.

The Need for Minorities in School Counseling

The Transforming School Counseling Initiative (TSCI) is a recent effort to bring school counselors

---

Charles Hanson is a professor of educational psychology at California State University, Northridge; Carolyn Stone is an associate professor of counselor education at the University of North Florida.

into the national initiative to improve teaching and learning. School counselors can be quite influential in the lives of students, impacting their aspirations, pushing them to high levels of achievement, and assisting them in developing career goals and educational plans. Minority school counselors can extend this influence by serving as role models for minority students and by exemplifying success in higher education and professional status in the community (Eubanks & Weaver, 1999). Minority school counselors are also more likely to know and understand the barriers to learning that minority students encounter and the support they need to forge paths of educational attainment and success. School counselors of color can also be a valuable resource to the school community in bridging the cultural gap between the school environment and students' home/community environments (Eubanks & Weaver, 1999).

The need for increasing the number of minority school counselors is evident. Addressing this need is critical if schools are to be effective in raising the academic achievement and college aspirations of minority students. The TSCI has moved this challenge forward by targeting the recruitment and selection processes of school counselor preparation programs for change.

Recruiting for Diversity

Recruiting for diversity is critical. We contend that minority and low socioeconomic status (SES) educators who have encountered and overcome institutional, systemic, and personal barriers to achievement have personal experiences that can lead to identifying, understanding, and eliminating those barriers for students from similar backgrounds. Minority and low SES school counselors are more likely to have confronted segregating educational issues such as low expectations of teachers, counselors, and school administrators; minimally prepared and unprepared teachers; schools with limited educational resources; and high school courses and programs that do not prepare students for college. Their experiences, as well as their close connections with minority and low-income families and students, make these counselors ideally suited to transform school counseling programs in ways that increase learning and academic achievement for all students.

With the TSCI, six university programs initiated extensive outreach recruitment efforts to find applicants with the skills, attitudes, and knowledge needed to match their mission statements and new vision programs, and to attract minority candidates. All six worked collaboratively with personnel from their local school districts (i.e., school counselors, teachers, administrators, family center directors) and community representatives (i.e., government leaders, community agency directors) in recruitment efforts. Recruitment goals varied across sites, but all TSCI university programs tried to recruit more minority students. Three sites set specific objectives related to this goal. One site set a target of 50% minority representation in the cohort of selected students in the first year of the project, with 60% representation in the second and subsequent years. Another site aimed to increase the number of students admitted to their program from 30 to 40 to 50 with a target of 1/3 minority representation. A third site set a goal of 30% minority representation in the first year, with 50% representation in the second and subsequent years. The remaining sites established more general goals of increasing the diversity in their selected group of applicants with one site also targeting an increase in the number of male students. Diversity for some included increasing the number of candidates who had professional experience in schools (e.g., as teachers, paraprofessionals, or school administrators). Only one site expected applicants to have teaching experience, and this was because two years of teaching was included in the state's licensure requirements.

Recruitment and Selection Practices

School counseling preparation programs have accepted the historical orientation to mental health counseling, reflecting little concern for how school counselors address the academic achievement of students (Collison et al., 1998; Education Trust, 1997). Little or no value, therefore, has been placed on identifying applicants who would best serve that purpose. Six universities in the TSCI have changed their recruitment and selection procedures in ways that diminish this mental health focus, as well as the reliance on traditional academic criteria such as grade point averages and scores on the Graduate Record Examination for selection into graduate school. Educators in these preparation programs have sought to identify candidates whose personal/social consciousness skills would help increase access to and success in a rigorous academic program for all K-12 students.

This new vision holds that counselors must be able to identify how inequality exists in schools and work to remove institutional, systemic, and situational barriers to learning. Counselor candidates who are willing to challenge the status quo, use their critical thinking abilities, and be proactive in the promotion of student academic achievement will possess a core of attitudes, thinking, and behaviors that are fundamental to a new vision of school counseling. The six universities funded as a result of the TSCI highlighted these qualities as necessary for new applicants to their programs and developed selection procedures to identify these qualities in potential students. All six of the TSCI counselor education programs, with some variation across institutions, employed the recruitment and selection procedures described below.

Mission-driven recruitment

The six universities organized teams of university faculty, school personnel, community members, and parents to develop mission statements that would shape their programs. The teams examined the current status of school counseling—locally and nationally—through readings, surveys, and focus groups. The groups' energy, enthusiasm, experience, and knowledge resulted in the development of comprehensive statements of mission and purpose that set the course and direction for the six programs. The six university preparation programs' mission statements reflected the need for school counselors to (a) focus on student achievement and remove barriers to student learning; (b) advocate for high-quality education for all students; and (c) become leaders in educational reform.

Recruitment activities

TSCI programs developed a multiplicity of recruitment activities. All sites developed or revised informational material to feature program mission statements, a new vision for future school counselors, and qualities desired in applicants. Application materials included program mission and vision statements. Some sites developed flyers and posters about their programs. Brochures were developed or revised and disseminated around university campuses, mailed to schools, and distributed in local communities. Some sites also distributed information to local school superintendents, principals, counselors, and community leaders. One university program even initiated an extensive mailing to schools and districts throughout the state. Program information, including mission and vision statements, was also posted on Web sites at all universities, with plans to link sites to a central TSCI project Web site. Most of the six universities posted advertisements in school district and teachers' union newsletters and other publications.

All six universities solicited the help of school and university stakeholders in recruitment efforts. School personnel and community members involved in the six university programs were asked to identify individuals with desirable qualities and encourage their application. Several universities developed and disseminated nomination forms requesting the names of teachers and community members who demonstrated the qualities needed to be a "new vision" school counselor. Two universities were able to engage the consultation and recruitment services of their campus diversity center programs. Specialists in these programs suggested recruitment activities, promoted information on school counseling as a career, and actively recruited applicants through school and university contacts.

All six programs recruited undergraduate students enrolled in psychology, social work, and education classes. Equity-based departments, courses, and social groups on each campus (e.g., Pan African Studies, Chicano Studies, African American Cultural Clubs, Minority Students in Psychology Club) also received information visits by program faculty, and, in some cases, by minority students currently enrolled in the school counseling programs. Several universities reported success in eliciting the help of alumni in recruitment efforts. Two universities recruited at historically African American colleges and universities. One university specifically recruited teachers and school paraprofessionals (i.e., teacher's aides, tutors, after-school program coordinators). Two universities engaged in long-range recruitment efforts by talking about school counseling as a profession with middle and high school students and undergraduate students in other colleges and universities. One university, Ohio State, collaborated with the local teachers' union to attract minority teachers.

Each university further invited nominees and interested individuals to attend informational meetings and fairs, where they were given an overview of program reforms and details on the curriculum and admissions procedures. One university worked with the local media to recruit school counseling candidates on the nightly news for a week, and accompanied the recruitment effort with a phone bank in which counselors and university faculty provided information to callers.

Recruitment Results

Active recruitment efforts overall generated larger and more diverse pools of applicants than evidenced in prior years. University programs reported increased interest from potential candidates, providing an opportunity to dispense program information widely. Nearly all programs significantly increased the number of applicants, with some programs attaining more than 60% increases in the first year. After two years, three universities had increased applications by over 100%. Not only were the numbers of applications increased, but all programs reported higher quality applicants overall.

The increase in the number of male and minority student applications universities received was impressive. A need for males to serve as role models exists, yet many universities have reported difficulty in recruiting men to the school counseling program. Recruitment efforts developed by the TSCI proved effective in drawing more men to university programs. Males now comprise over 30% of the candidates at two universities, and all six universities reported increases in the number of males applying to their programs during a two-year period.

Minority applicants and selected candidates have also grown significantly, with all programs seeing an increase. Several universities increased the number of minority candidates to over 50% of the student body, with one university attaining more than 70% minority students in the first year alone.

The recruitment data demonstrate that proactive efforts to increase the number and diversity of applicant pools to school counseling programs will be successful. In addition, recruitment success appears to be related to the energy and vision generated by university programs collaborating with local school districts and communities.

Selection Results

Selection results for the six university sites during the first two years of the project show some interesting outcomes (see Table 1). The numbers for Fall 1998 reflect the makeup of the student population at all TSCI university sites prior to the initiation of the project and implementation of new recruitment and selection procedures. The total number of students enrolled in all six programs increased approximately 32%, from 123 students in Fall 1998 to 162 students in Fall 2000. Most programs aimed to increase the number of students admitted as part of their project goals and were successful.

The number of students classified as full-time students showed an increase of 119% over two years, from 57 students enrolled full-time in Fall 1998 to 125 students in Fall 2000. The number of students enrolled part-time decreased 44 percent during this same period, from 66 students in Fall 1998 to 37 students in Fall 2000. These numbers may indicate greater commitment on the part of students to completing their educational preparation and entering the field. However, they may also reflect the students' commitment at the start of their program, but some students were not able to maintain a full-time commitment through their entire graduate school preparation. University faculty generally recognize that full-time graduate study places stress on students, particularly those from low-income backgrounds who may need to maintain gainful employment to support themselves and family members. Minority students also reported experiencing stress. Therefore, flexibility in program options, including part-time and full-time, was important to attract and retain these students.

The number of minority students admitted into all six TSCI sites increased substantially over the first two years of the project. Between Fall 1998 and Fall 2000, the number of African American students

Table 1
Enrollment Figures for Six TSCI Universities

	Fall 1998	Fall 1999	Fall 2000	Percent Change
Cohort Descriptors				
Number of students at the 6 university sites	123	136	162	31.7%
Number of full-time students	57	105	125	119.3%
Number of part-time students	66	31	37	-44%
Student Demographics				
African American	16	31	37	131.3%
Latino	4	11	12	200%
Other	1	3	4	300%
Euramerican/Caucasian	99	84	100	1%
Asian American	3	7	3	0%
Male	13	17	22	69.2%
Female	110	119	140	27.3%

Source: R. House (personal communication, January 2001)

increased 131%, with only 16 students admitted for Fall 1998, 31 students admitted for Fall 1999, and 37 admitted for Fall 2000.

The number of Latino students admitted to programs increased by 20% over the first two project years. In Fall 1998 programs reported only 4 Latino students. This increased to 11 Latino students in Fall 1999 and 12 students in Fall 2000. The increase in Latino students was seen primarily at California State University at Northridge (CSUN). CSUN has a large Latino population enrolled at the university, and Latinos comprise the majority population in local schools. Other TSCI universities have also seen increased numbers of Latinos in their communities and are actively recruiting Latino applicants.

Interestingly, the number of male students admitted to programs increased 69% in two years. Only 13 males were represented in the student groups of the six university sites before the start of the TSCI project in Fall 1998. This number increased to 17 by Fall 1999 and to 22 by Fall 2000. It appears that the efforts of university programs to recruit more male students were largely successful, although the total number of male students in these school counseling programs remains considerably lower than the number of female students.

A More Equitable Selection Procedure

In the past, the six TSCI universities relied heavily on standardized tests and/or grade point averages as indicators of a student's potential for success academically and as a future counselor. This narrowly focused approach was biased in favor of applicants who excelled in academics and left little room to consider an applicant's other personal strengths and characteristics. The new selection procedures reduce bias in the following ways: (a) Selection Team members approach the task seriously, and, because the total team makes the final decision, there are multiple voices determining an applicant's status; (b) multiple indicators are used, and at least two and as many as five Selection Team members can speak with knowledge about each applicant after having read his or her portfolio, conducting an interview, or listening to the applicant's speech (current graduate students also contribute to candidate evaluation); (c) a candidate is rejected by Selection Team members only when the decision is unanimous or the argument for rejection is convincing; and (d) applicants are rarely rejected outright as Selection Team members offer applicants ways to improve their application and an opportunity to reapply. Although, these selection procedures are imperfect, applicants reported that varied approaches made them believe they had an equal opportunity to be chosen.

Conclusion

Collaborative recruitment and selection efforts that include school district personnel, parents, and community members require an initial investment of time and effort devoted to building these relationships. The investment up front appears to generate payoffs as counselor educators obtain support and commitment to the recruitment, selection, and training of new school counselors.

Specific action focused on recruiting minority students to school counseling programs appears to be effective overall. Efforts supporting targeted goals appear most effective. The recruitment methods used by the six TSCI universities serve as a model for others. Program mission statements were particularly useful in both recruitment efforts and in attracting a new type of student who is committed to raising the academic achievement of all students and is willing to lead educational reform.

Findings from initial efforts at recruitment point to the need to build programs based on a vision for school counseling, to inform prospective applicants about the program, and to identify the qualities and experiences that characterize a good match between program and applicant. Selection procedures that embrace qualitative characteristics and the experiences of applicants can generate a diverse group of talented students. School counseling preparation programs that prepare professionals to make an impact on the lives of all students will attract high quality applicants.

References

Arredondo, P. (1999). Multicultural counseling competencies as tools to address oppression and racism. *Journal of Counseling and Development, 77*, 102-108.

Arredondo, P., Toporek, R., Brown, S.P., Jones, J., Locke, D.C., Sanchez, J., & Stadler, H. (1996). Operationalization of the multicultural counseling competencies. *Journal of Multicultural Counseling & Development, 24*, 42-78.

Brotherton, S.J. (1996). *Counselor education for the twenty-first century.* Westport, CT: Bergin & Garvey.

Collison, B.B., Osborne, J.L., Gray, L.A., House, R.M., Firth, J., & Lou, M. (1998). Preparing counselors for social action. In C.C. Lee & G.R. Walz (Eds.), *Social action: A mandate for counselors* (pp. 263-277). Alexandria, VA: American Counseling Association.

Council for the Accreditation of Counseling and Related Educational Programs. (1994). *CACREP accreditation standards and procedures manual.* Alexandria, VA: Author.

D'Andrea, M., & Arredondo, P. (1999). Promoting human dignity and development through diversity. *Counseling Today, 41*(10), 16, 22.

Dinsmore, J.A., & England, J.T. (1996). A study of multicultural counseling training at CACREP-accredited counselor education programs. *Counselor Education and Supervision, 36*(1), 58-76.

Education Trust, The. (1997, February). *The national guidance and counseling reform program.* Washington, DC: Author.

Eubanks, S.C., & Weaver, R. (1999). Excellence through diversity: Connecting the teacher quality and teacher diversity agendas. *The Journal of Negro Education, 68*, 451-459.

Hart, P., & Jacobi, M. (1992). *From gatekeeper to advocate: Transforming the role of the school counselor.* New York: College Entrance and Examination Board.

Herring, R.D. (1997). *Multicultural counseling in schools: A synergetic approach.* Alexandria, VA: American Counseling Association.

Lee, C.C. (Ed.). (1995). *Counseling for diversity: A guide for school counseling and related professions.* New York: Allyn & Bacon.

National Center for Educational Statistics. (1997). *America's teachers: Profile of a profession* (NCES 97-460). Washington, DC: U.S. Department of Education, Office of Educational Research and Improvement.

Orfield, G., & Yun, J.T. (1999). *Resegregation in American schools.* Cambridge, MA: Civil Rights Project of Harvard University.

Sue, E.W., Arredondo, P., & McDavis, R.J. (1992). Multicultural counseling competencies: A call to the profession. *Journal of Counseling and Development, 70*, 477-486.

Young, R.L., Chamley, J.D., & Withers, C. (1990). Minority faculty representation and hiring practices in counselor education programs. *Counselor Education and Supervision, 29*, 148-154.

Richard L. Hayes
Pamela O. Paisley

Transforming School Counselor Preparation Programs

TRANSFORMING THE EDUCATION of school counselors to prepare them to become educational leaders who serve as advocates for the equitable treatment of all children demands a systems-oriented approach. Transformed school counselors, unlike their predecessors who were schooled in individual and small-group interventions on behalf of selected students, will necessarily understand persons, groups, and organizations as complex systems that are embedded in a sociocultural context.

Meeting the demand to restructure school counselor education raises a set of challenging questions about ourselves as counselors and educators, about the content of our courses, and about our preferred teaching strategies. In addressing the broad concepts associated with program design, Paisley and Benshoff (1998) have suggested that transforming counselor education programs must involve a review of (a) the rationale for and the basic assumptions that underlie the proposed program; (b) the content of the curriculum and its program structure; (c) teaching methodologies; and (d) program evaluation. Further, the transformation of school counselor education will require an intentionality on the part of program faculty that demands the careful integration of theory and practice in program structure, curriculum development, and summative evaluation (Hoshmond & Polkinghorne, 1992; Rest, 1986).

In particular, we believe that transforming school counselor education from an individual-oriented to a systems-oriented approach will require that we not only broaden the scope of our curriculum (e.g., by adding new content related to schools and communities as systems), but that we also reconceptualize the very nature of instruction to reflect our present understanding of learning as both personally and contextually situated. Further, living in today's rapidly changing, technologically sophisticated, multicultural society demands that we prepare our students to be self-reflective, life-long learners who recognize that present knowledge is merely a temporary solution to the enduring problems of living life effectively.

We present the ideas in this article from the perspective of having been participants in restructuring our own school counseling master's degree program. Our commitment has been to apply what we know about human and organizational development to the education of counselors, and to enhance the lives of their clients as active participants in complex social systems (Hayes, Dagley, & Horne, 1996; Paisley & Hubbard, 1994). In this article, we address the underlying assumptions and values that guide our work, and we outline the components of our program that can serve as examples for translating theoretical principles into practice.

Richard L. Hayes and Pamela O. Paisley are professors of education at The University of Georgia.

We do not claim to have "the true path" for all counselor educators to follow in transforming school counselor education. We do, however, claim a "direction" that is consistent with the principles espoused in this *TIP* issue and with our own personal and professional experiences in promoting the development of our students and their clients. In asserting these beliefs, we acknowledge that our program may not be suitable for every counselor educator or everyone who wants to be a school counselor.

Basic Assumptions

Transforming our school counselor preparation program required that we reexamine our core values, remind ourselves of the central purposes of our work as counselors, recognize the roles we play as participants in schools as social systems, and acknowledge what we believe about teaching and learning. Despite being willing collaborators on a 4-person program faculty in a graduate department of 15 tenure-track faculty, we are not of one mind concerning the fine details of our theorizing about development and change. Nonetheless, we all accept that we have a central responsibility to prepare school counselors capable of the level of abstract thought, complex problem solving, and self-reflective practice necessary to work in today's schools and who are capable of sustaining the self-renewal necessary to transform themselves into the practitioner for recurrently emerging tomorrows. The contribution that we make as counselor educators to the communities in which we live is reflected ultimately in the quality of the service provided by our students. As such, we are interested in preparing counselors who are up to the challenge of being effective social change agents, in enhancing the lives of every child in school, and in improving the world community.

When we think of the best students we have had or the best counselors we have known, certain descriptors repeat themselves. These individuals tend to be flexible, tolerant of ambiguity, comfortable with a wide range of emotions, open-minded, self-directed yet collaborative, and enthusiastic learners. They trust themselves and others in new learning situations and seek the best in every relationship. They embrace diversity and can be critical as well as creative thinkers. And they are passionate about effecting social change that is personally and institutionally empowering. We believe that selecting such individuals at the outset for admission holds the greatest promise for preparing the kind of counselors we ultimately would like to graduate from our program. Further, we have some evidence that the higher the level of these qualities among the students we have admitted, the more likely the students are to achieve the goals of our program (Weitzman-Swain, 1995). We believe it is important in transforming the curriculum to consider fully the kind of person you really want to attract (as opposed to the kind you might otherwise attract or be assigned) to your program and what you need to offer them in the process of their transformation.

A greater challenge for us has been to decide what to do with the students during the two years they are with us. What activities will extend their considerable life experience in meaningful ways? What environments will build upon the knowledge, skills, and attitudes that inform their lives to this point? What type of educators will we have to be in order to realize our vision for their further development (as well as our own) as counseling professionals? How can we help them develop the skills, knowledge, and attitudes that will best serve them in becoming educational leaders who can act as advocates for all children?

In addressing these questions and in transforming our program, we have been guided by five basic assumptions:

1. Human development forms the basic conceptual framework for counseling theory and practice. Although past counselor education models have stressed the necessity of conceptualizing counseling practice in developmental terms (Borders & Drury, 1992; Paisley & Hubbard, 1994), our effort is to use what we know about human development to structure not only the curriculum but also the experience of our graduate students. In constructing both content and process, we have been guided by several theoretical models that are united by a constructivist perspective (Hayes & Oppenheim, 1997).[1]

2. Experience is not just the best teacher; it is the only teacher. We believe that people will practice *as* they were taught as opposed to *what* they were taught. We accept the responsibility to vary our teaching methodologies both cognitively and contextually to engage our students as participants in their own education. Further, building on what we know about necessary components for promoting development (Sprinthall & Thies-Sprinthall, 1983), we must assure that the experiences are significant and challenging and are accompanied by opportunities for reflection and support.

3. Group work provides the natural vehicle for social construction and for encouraging collaboration in the empowerment of our students. Small-group interaction can help build the sense of community necessary for a comprehensive school counselor preparation program while also grounding the development of our students in a team-oriented and collaborative approach to practice. Moreover, a whole set of contemporary issues calls for training in effective group work, including participatory decision making, multiculturalism, family systems, school restructuring, and community building.

4. Psychological concepts themselves can be taught as a means to promote human development. We are committed to this primary principle of deliberate psychological education (Mosher & Sprinthall, 1971), and to the corollary challenge for counselor educators to serve as architects for appropriate educational experiences to enhance developmental advancement.

5. Learning to use available technologies has become a vital life skill, and embracing change in the application of technology to the problems of work and daily living has become an essential attitude for surviving and thriving in the 21st century. We believe that technology can be used as an information resource, a communication tool, and as a mechanism for data collection, analysis, and dissemination in order to advocate for individual students or groups of students.

Using these assumptions regarding human development, experiential learning, group work, deliberate psychological education, and the supportive use of technology as a framework for curriculum development, we have endeavored to create a curriculum that takes a systems-oriented approach, is consistent with a developmental/constructivist perspective, and responds to the demand for school counselors who can enhance their own and others' development in today's society. In the sections that follow, we describe our model for program design related to selecting content for the curriculum, sequencing activities, and evaluating intended outcomes.

Content and Structure of the Curriculum

Our program is accredited by the Council for the Accreditation of Counseling and Related Educational Programs (CACREP). As such, we use the CACREP standards as guidelines for the basic content of professional preparation, and we require coursework in basic helping skills, human development, lifestyle and career development, cross-cultural counseling, group work, individual assessment, research methods and design, counseling theories, and practicum and internship. A core content is required across program specialties (e.g., school and community counseling) as agreed on by departmental faculty. As a school counseling faculty, we also use the Standards for Practice of the American School Counselor Association (ASCA) as a guide to content and practice in school counseling. Individual teaching style, instructional methodologies, classroom activities, and forms of evaluation are left to the academic integrity and creativity of the instructors.

Despite our recognition of the necessity to ground our students in the content of a professional education, we are aware that it is process and not content that drives the group work that underlies our curriculum development. As such, we have attempted to organize our curriculum to maximize growth-oriented interpersonal experiences and demonstration of emerging competencies in seven core areas of our transformation. Specifically, students are expected to demonstrate their competence in (a) counseling, (b) consultation and coordination, (c) multiculturalism, (d) teaming and collaboration, (e) advocacy, (f) leadership, and (g) use of technology to facilitate change.

The Cohort System

Consistent with the assumptions outlined previously, we have centered our restructured program around group work with a cohort of students. A cohort system allows students to enroll in the program as a group and remain together until completion. A new cohort is admitted to graduate study annually to undertake a two-year, structured sequence of courses. Our rationale for the cohort system, unlike that of many other disciplines that use similar programs, is not "administrative convenience," although it does offer that. Instead, we use this system as a more authentic context for learning, as a supportive environment that provides role-taking opportunities and ongoing dialogue with others, and as a place for guided reflection on the experiences of graduate preparation.

The cohort also provides a vehicle for students to negotiate interpersonal and organizational issues over a sustained period. Aware of the chronic lament of developmental interventionists that "significant change might have been realized had we had more time," we have committed ourselves from the outset to a period of two calendar years. Such an extended period not only allows for sustained contact among the faculty and students, but it permits the student cohort sufficient time to develop into the type of learning community that can begin to direct its own education. Further, the use of a cohort group of master's students creates the expectation that they ought to collaborate with others and provides a model for building an empowered professional counseling staff once employed (Goodlad, 1990; Human Services Policy Center, 1992; Su, 1990).

Building the cohort

Community building begins with the admissions process. As Collison (1998) cautions: "Admission begins with mission" (p. 1). We have been careful to describe our program and its guiding vision for counselor education to prospective students. In being forthright about the type of program we have and the type of student we are looking for, we believe we have been able to more often attract the kind of student we want. More importantly, we also create an anticipatory mindset that both challenges and encourages our students to realize these goals. Following a paper review of each applicant's materials to assess previous academic performance (e.g., GRE, GPA, MAT scores), their personality and work habits as assessed by others (e.g., letters of reference), their commitment to graduate education (e.g., personal essay), and their level of cognitive development (e.g., transcript, personal essay), we invite 20-24 of the most promising and diverse set of applicants to our campus for a day of interviews. Two groups of 10-12 each join us for a series of group and individual interviews. The day consists of a group orientation, individual interviews, and a small-group experience. The group orientation provides a basis for applicants' informed consent concerning continued interest in our program. Faculty members outline the program philosophy, requirements, and procedures.

Applicants also participate in two individual interviews with faculty members and a small-group activity with the program coordinator. While waiting for these individual interviews, applicants meet informally as members of an open group with doctoral students affiliated with the program and with currently enrolled master's students. This process provides a less structured setting within which to assess students on a variety of dimensions critical to their success in the program. We consider the interview day not only as a time for the program faculty to make final admissions decisions, but also for students to decide if the program is the best match for them. Consistent with our view of reality as socially constructed, these interviews provide an early opportunity for everyone to test emerging assumptions.

Although we cannot get a complete picture of every student under such abbreviated circumstances, we do look for confirming evidence of a set of personal characteristics consistent with the goals of our program. In particular, we try to assess the students on as many of the following characteristics as possible: (a) level of self-awareness; (b) capacity for self-reflection; (c) natural interest in and awareness of others; (d) interpersonal, coping, and learning styles; (e) areas of potential bias incompatible with program objectives; (f) obvious prejudices (e.g., racism, sexism); (g) previous experience with persons of another culture; (h) awareness of self and impact on others; (i) appropriate level of self-disclosure; (j) honest commitment to diversity; (k) capacity to profit from and contribute to a group-oriented curriculum; (l) sense of humor, especially about oneself; (m) willingness to take risks interpersonally; and (n) flexibility and toleration of ambiguity.

As comprehensive as this list may appear, we recognize that people are complex and reveal themselves in multiple ways in selected circumstances. Our effort in these interviews is to provide a broad range of opportunities, with multiple audiences, for applicants to reveal themselves to us. The faculty and doctoral students then discuss all applicants until a consensus is reached about their prospects for success in the program and about the overall makeup of the cohort as a whole. In particular, we attempt to create both the most diverse group of students to foster cognitive dissonance and promote interpersonal development, while also selecting persons who are likely to both contribute to and thrive in such a challenging environment. Ten to 12 applicants are ultimately invited for admission to the program and, based on our experience of the past few years, virtually all will accept.

Sequencing the Curriculum

As noted above, the curriculum consists of a planned six-semester sequence of courses (two calendar years beginning in June) through which the students progress as a cohort. In classes taught by the program faculty (e.g., foundations of school counseling, professional development seminar, practicum, and internship), students are grouped and regrouped in collaborative problem-solving task groups as a means of providing the challenge and support necessary to development. Unused to working together, however, each new cohort of master's students encounters interpersonal and cross-cultural problems that require new ways of relating. A benefit of these problem-solving experiences is to enhance students' capacities to interact and help them to overcome the cultural (Su, 1990) and professional (Lortie, 1975) issues that are widespread characteristics of counselors' lives. Toward these ends, we have adopted a team development model for sequencing the curriculum.

The sequence of courses is framed using the team development tasks under the rubrics of awareness, conflict, cooperation, productivity, and separation, as outlined by Kormanski and Mozenter (1987). During the first of their six semesters in the program, students take the basic counseling theories course with a helping skills lab, a cross-cultural counseling course, and a foundations of school counseling course, where they are introduced to our assumptions and to the new vision for school counseling in detail. In the foundations course, students also begin work on the platform for a Web-based portfolio, a project extending across the two years of the program. In addition, they participate in a week-long professional development workshop with second-year students and collaborating counselors from area schools. The workshop introduces them to multicultural counseling and to teamwork, while also introducing them to the use of computer technology for information retrieval (e.g., Internet searches, university library, ERIC) and communications (e.g., e-mail, PowerPoint, WebCT) in addressing a real world problem in partnership with a collaborating school counselor. These courses provide a strong basis for grounding students in the profession and provide opportunities for them to better understand themselves, each other, and the real world of a professional school counselor. This first semester is focused on developing students' awareness of themselves and others and on their emerging understanding of what it means to be a professional counselor. The intended outcomes are a commitment to the broad values and goals of the program and of the field and acceptance of themselves and one another as members of a diverse cohort.

During the second semester, students take 8-11 credit hours of coursework, including courses in individual assessment and career theories as well as a school counseling seminar. The second semester usually gives rise to some predictable interpersonal conflict. Team building at this stage of the curriculum includes acknowledging and confronting the conflict and listening with understanding to the reasons that underlie stated differences. The use of technology continues as students learn to use computerized instruments for individual and school-wide assessment and expand their knowledge of available resources on the Internet. Whenever possible, students work together as members of a team, sharing ideas and developing projects using the computer as a facilitative tool. Desired outcomes for this stage are clarification of their roles and expectations for the group, and a sense of belonging.

In the third semester, students complete studies in career applications and group work, complete a practicum, and continue in the school counseling seminar. The third semester continues the tasks of promoting cooperation through open communication and increasing cohesion among the members. As before, the computer is used to facilitate their communications with one another about in-class activities and to retrieve and analyze data. Further, they are introduced to the extensive world of career-planning materials available on the Internet and engage in collaborative career development projects with school counselors as part of their practicum. At this writing, we have just begun the use of split-screen video technology to evaluate group leadership and to assess interpersonal awareness in counseling across cultures. The desired outcomes of this semester are involvement by everyone in the work of the group and support for one another in reaching mutually determined goals. Particularly in the context of the practicum, students become increasingly problem-focused as members encourage one another to contribute ideas and solutions. In this working stage of the group's development, productivity emerges as a central theme as students realize a sense of achievement with their clients and a growing pride in their work as counselors.

The fourth semester includes courses in research and developmental counseling as well as completion of program electives. We require guided electives in (a) educational leadership, (b) educational psychology, and (c) families, schools, and communities. The research course, as well as the guided electives, are taught outside the department with collaborating faculty in teacher education, educational leadership, and social work. Collaborative projects with graduate students from other programs reinforce the need for interdisciplinary collaboration and further the development of a systems-oriented approach to counseling practice.

The final two semesters involve a half-time internship placement and an ongoing professional seminar. This period further refines the work of the cohort as a team. Problems once thought to be simple are now recognized as complex and as demanding a systemic approach to their solution. In the internship seminar, goals are broken down by objectives, subgroups are formed to work on related tasks, and milestones are established both to motivate team members and to serve as points for celebration.

The sixth and final semester is focused intentionally on issues of separation for the cohort. Recognizing and rewarding team efforts become central objectives at this time. Students are encouraged to express their appreciation of one another and to share their experience of having been a member of the cohort for the past two years. As a final assignment, students complete the work on their Web-based portfolios, which present summaries of their professional work to date, examples of products resulting from their study, and relevant supporting documentation for review by potential employers. Several opportunities are provided for processing their experiences and accomplishments, both formally (through in-class activities and an individual exit interview) and informally (through activities at a graduation party).

Evaluation

In intentionally designing a graduate program to promote development as well as provide content knowledge and skill development, we realized that our program evaluation would require special attention. If we accept promoting development as a goal for counselor preparation, then program evaluation needs to assess related variables (Lusky & Hayes, 2001; Paisley & Benshoff, 1998). Rest (1986) suggested the construction of a research agenda for assessing development that would include relevant instruments to (a) appraise entering students; (b) evaluate the effectiveness of educational programs; and (c) ascertain the competence of and developmental status of graduating professionals.

Using this model, we have been interested not only in the traditional student satisfaction reports and assessments of student competency in counseling, but also in changes in levels of development and in-depth qualitative reports of the students' experiences in the program. In particular, we have attempted to assess their facility in counseling, consultation, and coordination—especially with diverse clients—their skills in advocacy and leadership—especially in group work and team-oriented activities—and their use of technology as a tool for information management as well as data analysis in disaggregation of school-wide data for program evaluation. Therefore, we use a multifaceted approach to capture both the outcomes and relevant processes.

All students complete a quantitative survey of satisfaction as well as a comprehensive examination related to the core and specialty content areas. The comprehensive examination is a multiple-choice exam modeled after the National Counselor Exam. The satisfaction survey uses a Likert scale to assess the adequacy of preparation and a ranking to determine the significance of various aspects of the program in preparing them to be effective in their current work site. On this form, students are specifically asked to provide a numerical rating and narrative feedback evaluating their practicum and internship experiences and the effectiveness of the supervision they received. In addition to these paper and pencil assessments, each student completes an exit interview with one of the doctoral students affiliated with the program. The exit interviews are usually 1-2 hours in length and consist of 15 open-ended questions about student experiences. These interviews are taped and then reviewed qualitatively by a departmental research team looking for themes and for deeper understandings of the quantitative results. Aside from assessment data, the exit interviews provide an excellent method for student reflection on the experience of graduate preparation and a natural vehicle for closure. In addition, doctoral students affiliated with our school research team have developed specific interview protocols to assess student experiences within the cohort related to multicultural awareness, self-reflection, the decision to enroll, and knowledge and skill competencies consistent with the new vision. Students are also asked to develop a Web-based portfolio documenting their experiences and competencies in all program areas.

Program evaluation and analysis of data is ongoing. We use the results to inform our restructuring of both the process and content of our curriculum. Because we recognize that the preparation program is continually co-constructed with our students, we also acknowledge that the ever-changing nature of the two years creates a unique experience for each cohort.

We are aware of the challenges attendant on the creation of a constructive-developmental, deliberate psychological education model that purports to enhance personal and professional development in the preparation of self-reflective practitioners. This goal is especially challenging when we intend that they should function as educational leaders who will serve as advocates on behalf of all children in complex, multicultural systems. In particular, we recognize that implementation of such a curriculum is an ongoing, iterative process that demands constant attention. We have learned that this kind of program development is very difficult. It is time-consuming, has few immediate rewards, demands extraordinary patience, and tests our commitment to closely cherished values about democratic involvement, participatory decision making, honoring diverse perspectives, and the need as counselors to be empathic and understanding. More than anything, it demands a sophisticated use of the larger system's resources and a commitment to the process of collaborative inquiry. We also, however, have known the personal challenge, excitement, and reward the process brings. We often find ourselves stretched beyond our current capacity for teaching and learning, and yet grateful to be on this journey with our colleagues and our students.

Note

1. In particular, we accept a developmental perspective that is informed by Piaget's (1936/1954) approach to genetic epistemology, Kelly's (1955) personal construct theory, Kohlberg's (1969) theory of moral development, Dewey's (1916/1944) educational philosophy, Mead's (1934) theory of symbolic interactionism, and a system-oriented approach first articulated by Bertalanffy (1968).

References

Bertalanffy, L. (1968). *General system theory: Foundations, development, applications.* New York: Braziller.

Borders, L.D., & Drury, S.M. (1992). Comprehensive school counseling programs: A review for policymakers and practitioners. *Journal of Counseling and Development, 70,* 487-498.

Collison, B. (1998, January). *Active admissions: You get what you look for.* Paper presented at the annual meeting of The Education Trust, Inc., Washington, DC.

Dewey, J. (1944). *Democracy and education.* New York: Free Press. (Original work published 1916)

Goodlad, J. (1990). Studying the education of educators: From conception to findings. *Phi Delta Kappan, 70*(9), 698-701.

Hayes, R.L., Dagley, J.C., & Horne, A.M. (1996). Restructuring school counselor education: Work in progress. *Journal for Counseling and Development, 74,* 378-384.

Hayes, R.L., & Oppenheim, R. (1997). Constructivism: Reality is what you make it. In T. Sexton & B. Griffin (Eds.), *Constructivist thinking in counseling practice, research, and training* (pp. 19-40). New York: Teachers College, Columbia University Press.

Hoshmond, L., & Polkinghorne, D. (1992). Redefining the science-practitioner relationship and professional training. *American Psychologist, 47,* 55-56.

Human Services Policy Center. (August 1992). *Training for interprofessional collaboration for client responsive, integrated services.* Unpublished manuscript, University of Washington, Seattle.

Kelly, G.A. (1955). *The psychology of personal constructs.* New York: Norton.

Kohlberg, L. (1969). Stage and sequence: The cognitive-developmental approach to socialization. In D. Goslin (Ed.), *Handbook of socialization theory and research* (pp. 347-480). Chicago: Rand McNally.

Kormanski, C., & Mozenter, A. (1987). A new model of team building: A technology for today and tomorrow. *The 1987 annual: Developing human resources* (pp. 255-268). La Jolla, CA: University Associates.

Lortie, D. (1975). *Schoolteacher: A sociological study.* Chicago: University of Chicago Press.

Lusky, M., & Hayes, R.L. (2001). Collaborative consultation and program evaluation. *Journal of Counseling & Development, 79,* 26-38.

Mead, G.H. (1934). *Mind, self, and society.* Chicago: University of Chicago Press.

Mosher, R., & Sprinthall, N. (1971). Psychological education: A means to promote personal development during adolescence. *The Counseling Psychologist, 2*(4), 3-82.

Paisley, P., & Benshoff, J. (1998). A developmental focus: Implications for counselor education. *Canadian Journal of Counselling, 32,* 27-36.

Paisley, P., & Hubbard, G. (1994). *Developmental school counseling programs: From theory to practice.* Alexandria, VA: ACA.

Piaget, J. (1954). *The origins of intelligence in children.* New York: International Universities Press. (Original work published 1936)

Rest, J.R. (1986). *Moral development: Advances in research and theory.* New York: Praeger.

Sprinthall, N.A., & Thies-Sprinthall, L. (1983). The teacher as adult learner: A cognitive developmental view. In G. Griffin (Ed.), *Staff Development* (pp. 13-35). Chicago: National Society for the Study of Education.

Su, Z. (1990). The function of the peer group in teacher socialization. *Phi Delta Kappan, 70*(9), 723-727.

Weitzman-Swain, A. (1995). *The influence of interactive journal writing on the self-development, self-reflective ability, and empathy ratings of counselors in training.* Unpublished doctoral dissertation, University of Georgia, Athens.

C. Marie Jackson, Brent M. Snow, Susan R. Boes,
Paul L. Phillips, Rebecca Powell Stanard,
Linda C. Painter, Mary Beth Wulff

Inducting the Transformed School Counselor Into the Profession

NEW SCHOOL COUNSELOR education graduates from programs such as those developed through the Transforming School Counseling Initiative (TSCI) (Education Trust, 1997) have been prepared to facilitate learning opportunities for all students in a diverse environment. These TSCI graduates also have been prepared as leaders in attaining equitable opportunities for all students. According to House and Martin (1998) an increasingly global society calls for better use of resources and demands closing the achievement gap between poor and minority children and their more advantaged peers. This new vision developed through the TSCI has focused on the need to increase academic achievement and has acknowledged the role of counselors as change agents and advocates for the removal of barriers that impede student success. Thus, an academic focus must become the primary goal of these newly transformed school counselors. These new graduates will be faced with the challenge of entering a changing profession, not yet fully operational under the transformed models to which they have been introduced. Supporting these *transformed counselors* who are eager to implement their newly acquired attitudes,

knowledge, and skills will be necessary for implementation of the new vision. Never has it been more important to recognize that the early stages of induction to the profession are critical for the development of a lasting identity and continued growth of the school counseling profession.

Brott and Myers (1999) explored the professional identity development of counselors. According to these researchers, professional identity development is a process evolving over time, beginning during counselor training programs, and continuing throughout one's career. They discussed the process of transformation that takes place in determining a school counseling program. They described the school counselor's view of the counselor role as moving from an externally influenced one (influences such as the graduate training program) to a more internally influenced conceptualization of role. Literature relative to professional socialization and development cited by Brott and Myers (Hall, 1987; Watts, 1987) reported that one's early training in a profession is merely the beginning of professional growth and development. Ultimately, the counselor's role concept is determined by his or her individual personal guidelines evolving as the role is internalized on the job. These internalized personal guidelines may determine to a great extent what and how school counseling is delivered.

The findings of the Brott and Myers (1999) study supported the need for careful induction into

---

Brent M. Snow is professor, Linda C. Painter and Paul L. Phillips are associate professors, C. Marie Jackson, Susan R. Boes, Rebecca Powell Stanard, and Mary Beth Wulff are assistant professors of education at State University of West Georgia.

the profession (e.g., mentoring, new counselor academies, networking, attending professional conferences and seminars with others in and across the profession). An important implication of this study is "that counselors-in-training be prepared with a mindset that they will evolve and change in their professional role, that they will be made aware of the factors that impact their professional development, and that they will ultimately determine the counseling program and services offered in the school setting" (p. 346). Their findings underscore the value of preprofessional counselor training programs and mandate that counselor educators include decision-making opportunities through seminars related to issues in schools, and practical experiences for understanding relationships with the various stakeholders throughout the training program, especially during early clinical experiences.

Practicum and internship provide the first opportunities for counselors-in-training (CITs) to enter practice in the "real world." These clinical experiences within the curriculum encompass a significant portion of the student's academic experience. As counselor preparation programs are restructured to reflect the TSCI vision, clinical experiences must also be restructured to reflect the practices that have been integrated throughout the coursework. Changing the nature of these experiences must be done in order to align new "theory with practice." Supporting, supervising, and mentoring these CITs with an understanding of the challenges before them is a necessity. Borders and Leddick (1987) spoke of the early developmental stages of new counselors as times of dependency and imitation. It is quite normal for counselors in these early stages to be characterized by feelings of confusion, doubt, and internal conflict. VanZandt and Perry (1992) reported that the early stages of induction into the profession are critical. It seems even more so when the profession is in the midst of change.

The purpose of this article is to provide an overview of the importance and impact of the induction phase for graduates of TSCI programs and to provide a rationale for strengthening the involvement of counselor educators in this valuable process. We have included a review of literature and further discussion on (a) current practices in practicum and internship, (b) the mentoring process and supervision experiences, (c) the need to develop on-site supervisors, (d) the need for novice counselors to develop relationships with the various stakeholders, and (e) the continuing need for professional development for practicing school counselors.

Practicum and Internship
Practicum

Bradley and Fiorini (1999) assessed the status of practicum in counselor education programs. These researchers provided an overview of practicum in regard to curriculum content, assessment of quality, and the competencies required for completion of a beginning-level practicum. The results of their study indicated that the requirements for prerequisite coursework were similar among most programs. The content areas most likely to be prerequisites to practicum were theory and practice, professional orientation, human growth and development, and group work. When reviewing prerequisites, the researchers noted that there was no uniform requirement of a multicultural counseling course prior to practicum. In the reported data, 70% of the counselor educators stated that such a course was not required in their program, and yet 88% reported holding the expectation that practicum students would have the ability to work with clients from diverse cultures. The 2001 Council for the Accreditation of Counseling and Related Educational Programs (CACREP) standards do require that students in clinical experiences have the opportunity to counsel diverse clients. The skills necessary to meet the needs of diverse students are essential to the implementation of the new vision for school counseling (House & Martin, 1998; Jackson, Snow, Phillips, Boes, & Rolle, 1999; Snow, 2000).

Bradley and Fiorini (1999) reported as a concern that only 61% of the counselor educators surveyed in their study held the expectation that practicum students would be competent to demonstrate the ability to facilitate a group. Since CACREP defines practicum as including group work, this competency seems essential. Their study underscored the need to establish specific competencies for practicum students to achieve a readiness to assume the role expectations in internship and in the real world.

Results of a national survey (Perusse, Goodnough, & Noel, 2001) of counselor education programs with a clinical experience component supported that most programs require students to complete 100 hours of clinical experience in a school setting for practicum. However, there was a wide variation among all programs surveyed; only 55.9% provided prepracticum clinical experiences in a school setting prior to practicum, such as job shadowing, classroom observation, interviews with professionals, and various other projects. The TSCI vision supports the value of prepracticum in-school experiences for expanding the opportunity to practice the various skill components foundational to practicum and internship.

Internship

A review of the literature revealed little research relative to internship or clinical supervision of school counselors in training. Internship as a clinical experience component is defined more broadly than practicum. CACREP (2001) has defined it as a 600 clock-hour experience under the supervision of a certified school counselor. It is further designated to be "a distinctly defined, postpracticum, supervised 'capstone' clinical experience in which the student refines and enhances basic counseling or student development knowledge and skills and integrates and authenticates professional knowledge and skills appropriate to the student's program and initial postgraduate professional placement" (p. 103).

Suggested changes for clinical experiences

The new vision for school counseling has extended dimensions of the school counselor role in the arenas of leadership, advocacy, collaboration and brokering of services, and use of assessment data (Education Trust, 1997; Jackson et al., 1999; Snow, 2000). A collaborative community-school systemic approach to developing a comprehensive school counseling program is at the core of the TSCI. The school counselor who has been trained in this initiative is a key leader in the collaborative attainment of success for all students (Jackson et al., 2001). The recognition that the school counselor's role must focus on meeting the needs of all students through advocacy and leadership calls for a greater emphasis on group work than on individual counseling delivery. Clinical experiences must change to reflect a new way of doing things. The recommended preparation shift for the 21st-century role suggests more emphasis on brief counseling models—both individual and group—with a greater focus on group work, including small-group counseling, task groups, and large-group guidance. The CACREP 2001 standards state, "it is imperative that programs explicitly prepare students to be counselors first and counseling specialists second" (p. 55). The new vision for school counselors places an emphasis on the need for a school counseling specialist, one who removes barriers to academic achievement. However, in accord with CACREP guidelines, this specialist remains first and foremost, a skilled counselor using counseling skills to enhance learning and the academic environment.

Written plans for clinical experiences

Recommended changes in clinical experiences include the development of better communication between the intern, on-site supervisor, the site administrator, and the university supervising instructor in the collaborative planning of practicum and internship agreements. Practicum agreements should specify experiences in the use of brief approaches to both individual and group work. Collaboration, referral, and effective use of data are appropriate experiences for integration during the practicum. From the practicum experience, the transformed counselor gains the foundational skills needed for total role implementation within the internship experience.

A tentative plan describing how the intern will be involved in the various arenas of the newly transformed model—advocacy, leadership, collaboration and brokering of services, assessment and effective use of data, in addition to counseling—forms the basis of a helpful internship agreement. These arenas must be defined operationally so that CITs, supervisors, and administrators can implement and accurately target appropriate activities and assessments. Working with the site to develop this contractual plan would do more than solidify an agreement. It can also be an indirect means of providing professional development concerning the TSCI model. However, a more direct on-site training for the development of such an agreement, including examples of appropriately developed plans, would be beneficial. A workshop of this type could provide an opportunity to increase the knowledge of all those involved with the new vision for developing effective school counselors.

Curriculum-integrated clinical experiences

Another suggested change is the integration of various in-the-field experiences concurrent with the associated curriculum content, rather than as a single prepracticum class. For example, a counselor shadowing experience as part of an introductory course has been reported to be one of the best experiences required of students. Early clinical experiences coupled with appropriate curricular content can provide a hands-on opportunity to apply new knowledge. Other examples include sending students into the school to design and implement an advocacy project or, as part of leadership training, to observe and interview a broad range of school leaders—including counselors—to assess the leadership skills required in the various roles. These are ways of preparing the CITs for the culminating internship through early in-the-school experiences. In addition, early entry into the school provides an opportunity for them to better assess the appropriateness of their career choice before the end of their degree program.

The Nature of Mentoring and Supervision Experiences

A mentoring process can facilitate graduates' induction into the profession as they assume school counseling positions. However, finding the right mentor will be a critical factor. There will be a need for mentors who adhere to, and are knowledgeable of, the underpinnings of the various current educational reform agendas, such as the TSCI (Education Trust, 1997) and the National Standards for School Counseling Programs (Campbell & Dahir, 1997). Finding and maintaining contact with mentors who hold similar belief structures about the need to serve all students and support high academic achievement will be important for successful induction. As early as 1963 Munger, Myers, and Brown reported that appropriate counselor behaviors gained during the preparation program were often removed as a result of experience. Matthes (1992) stated that the importance of induction into the profession "cannot be stressed enough" when considering various factors such as the normal difficulty experienced when practicing new behaviors (p. 246). Knowing that mentors with a similar mind-set will not be plentiful, counselor educators must ensure that new graduates enter the field with (a) a thorough knowledge of the school counseling program mission, (b) a clear vision of a successfully implemented program, and (c) a firmly implanted understanding of the skills and attitudes to seek in a mentor. Finding a mentor to guide the implementation of a model focused on advocacy, high academic achievement for all students, and collaborative counseling relationships in the school and community may not be easy.

It is not likely that a formal system to align a new counselor with a veteran school counselor who shares this new vision will be available. VanZandt and Perry (1992) suggested a formal statewide mentoring program by using practicing school counselors. These authors addressed the difficulty of providing for such an effort, but recognized that professional counseling associations, certification boards, and universities who prepare counselors could provide this leadership. As part of establishing a formal induction process, a personal follow-up by professors of new graduates on the job can begin a monitoring process and could also lay the groundwork for collecting feedback on their successes and trials. In turn, this feedback can provide a basis for future curricular changes and professional development needs. In collaboration with P-12 school counselors, university counselor educators can further develop mentoring by providing a selection and training process. This process would enable seasoned school counselors to become mentors who are knowledgeable and supportive of the transformed roles and willing to provide ongoing peer supervision.

One example of a statewide mentoring project discussed in the literature was a collaborative project between the Maine School Counseling Association, the University of Southern Maine, and the Maine Department of Educational and Cultural Services (VanZandt & Perry, 1992). The final evaluation reported the project to be very worthwhile.

However, the major criticisms included problems arising from geographic location and matching of mentors with new counselors. One of the major benefits reported was simply having the knowledge that there was someone to call for support. Having someone with similar issues and concerns available for networking and mutual support seemed valuable. Therefore, arming the transformed counselor with an awareness of the qualities to look for when seeking a mentor where no formal program exists becomes critical to successful induction.

Time spent in training the preservice counselor in the qualities of a successful mentor is somewhat like "growing" mentors. As these graduates successfully implement a transformed counseling program they, in turn, become mentors for the next cohort group to be inducted into the profession. Encouraging ongoing peer supervision and providing supervision workshops, seminars, and continuing education opportunities for growth, discussion, and problem solving for counselors in the field will further enhance the induction of new counselors into the profession.

On-Site Supervision for School Counselors

The need for, and lack of, clinical supervision of school counselors has long been documented in the professional literature. Boyd and Walter (1975) noted that while school counselors, like counselors in other settings, need supervision in order to perform their duties adequately, often that supervision is lacking. More recent studies suggest that the situation has changed little (Borders & Usher, 1992; Roberts, 2001; Roberts & Borders, 1994). Borders and Usher, in a survey of Nationally Certified Counselors, found that school counselors reported significantly fewer hours of postdegree supervision than counselors in other settings, and almost half of the school counselors reported no postdegree counseling supervision at all. Typically principals or other administrators with little or no counseling background provide administrative supervision to school counselors, which does little or nothing to develop the clinical skills and professional identity of the novice counselor (Schmidt & Barret, 1983; Sutton & Page, 1994; Wilson & Remley, 1987). Researchers have reported several reasons for this lack of clinical supervision by counseling professionals, including lack of release time, financial support (Sutton & Page, 1994), and clinical supervision experience and skills (Henderson & Lampe, 1992). The lack of experience is not surprising given the fact that supervision training has always been considered more appropriate at levels beyond the master's level as reflected in CACREP standards (2001). However, the standards state that site supervisors should meet minimum master's degree requirements "in counseling or a related profession with equivalent qualification including appropriate certifications and/or licenses; a minimum of two years of pertinent professional experience in the area in which the student is completing clinical instruction; and knowledge of the program's expectations, requirements, and evaluation procedures for students" (Section III C.1-2 p. 66). Further, these standards call for school counseling interns to be under the supervision of a site supervisor as defined in the document.

Induction: Sinking or swimming

The lack of clinical supervision is particularly problematic for new graduates of transformed school counseling programs. While inexperienced, they will be expected from their first day on the job to assume the same responsibilities as experienced counselors (Matthes, 1992). Matthes calls it a "sink or swim" primary mode of induction (p. 248). This is particularly true for the transformed counselors. They may be employed in settings in which they are the only counselors on staff, or the other counselors have been trained in different models of service delivery. They will enter the profession with new competencies developed in the transformed school counseling training programs but without the guidance of supervisors familiar with the transformed role of the school counselor. It becomes incumbent on counselor educators to train experienced school counselors not only in clinical supervision skills but also in the essential elements of a transformed vision of school counseling in order to provide these new graduates with support. Peace and Sprinthall (1998) called for "the creation of systematic in-service programs to train experienced school counselors for the role of mentor and supervisor of beginning counselors" (p. 2). In-service training is supported by CACREP (2001) accreditation standards and is essential when implementing a new model such as that proposed by the TSCI.

Approaches to supervision training

Different approaches to supervision training of school counselors have been reported in the professional literature (Nelson & Johnson, 1999; Roberts, 2001) ranging from training as long as two semesters (Peace & Sprinthall, 1998) to as brief as four half-day training sessions (Henderson & Lampe, 1992). There are significant issues that must be considered when designing supervision training programs. For example, training programs must be designed using appropriate strategies for adult learners that focus on not only skill acquisition but also on constructivist growth (Peace & Sprinthall, 1998). Trainees must be introduced to supervision models, methods, and procedures as well as be provided an opportunity to practice supervision (Henderson & Lampe, 1992). Supervisors must be familiar with the principles of brief counseling, group facilitation, and various types of group work, including small-group counseling, task groups, and large-group guidance. In addition to providing skill-based supervision, supervisors must understand and champion the transformed role of the school counselor if they are to fully assist counselors trained in that model. Without this "new" vision of school counseling by supervisors, beginning counselors will struggle with both identity and role.

Relationships With the Important Stakeholders

A school counseling program does not belong to the school counselor alone (Gysbers & Henderson, 1994; Muro & Kottman, 1995; Myrick, 1993). The school counselor may be perceived as central to the school counseling program; however, a successful program cannot be implemented without the support and involvement of the members of the school and community. Knowing how to work with the various stakeholders (e.g., administrators, teachers, school staff, other counselors, parents, students, and community members) is essential to the implementation of a newly transformed school counseling program and to the successful induction of the newly trained counselor.

Teachers cannot concentrate solely on academic achievement in today's classrooms because they also must face the challenges of socialization, classroom management, and the physical and emotional development of students presently existing in schools. School counselors are often called on to consult with teachers on increasingly more complex issues (Shoffner & Briggs, 2001) and are usually expected to work collaboratively with all those concerned. Muro and Kottman (1995) discussed the importance of the manner in which the school counselor approaches this process, suggesting that the counselor should not take on the "expert" approach. Instead, the counselor should seek to help teachers develop their own skills in this area.

Johnson (2000) discussed the widespread lack of understanding on the part of educational administrators and classroom teachers of the role of the school counselor. She further suggested that it is important to help these professionals better understand the role. Many times the perceptions held about the role and effectiveness of the school counselor are largely determined by the administration. Administrators who see the job of the school counselor as one of administrative assistant or coordinator of scheduling, testing, records, and such, often institute that role. The school counselor will not be seen as an advocate or change agent within the school and community without administrative support of that role.

Historically, school counselors and principals have had little opportunity during their training for discussion of roles and learning about the perspectives and tasks of the other. Shoffner and Williamson (2000) suggested a format for a training seminar where both could meet for this purpose. Additionally, administrators might learn more about the programs school counselors are expected to initiate to meet the needs of today's complex issues. This type of seminar could be instrumental in preparing and motivating principals to better provide mentoring activities for new counselors within their schools, as well as simply improving the working relationships between the two groups through better understanding of differing perspectives.

The cultivation of a positive working relationship between the school counselor and principal is important to the emerging school counseling professional (Gysbers & Henderson, 1994; Vaught,

1995). Niebuhr, Niebuhr, and Cleveland (1999) promoted the collaborative roles of principal and counselors for the overall improvement of school climate. Often, principals do not fully understand the counseling program or how the counselor can contribute to student achievement and the overall climate of the school. Yet, according to Kaplan and Evans (1999), principals in today's schools view school counselors as leaders and integral partners in the education team more than ever. Through appropriate interaction and sharing of knowledge with principals, school counselors are in the position to foster their own successful induction into the school system. It is essential that the CIT curriculum address the counselor's collaborative role in the school and the community. Yet, beyond the curriculum, the university program has a responsibility to think creatively in regard to programs and projects to enhance school counselor relationships with the multiple publics holding an interest in student success.

The Change Process

The integration of new ideas into school counseling programs requires a rethinking of priorities, time, resources, and outcomes (Dahir, 2000). The novice counselor who has gained a sound foundation in program development and knows the mission and the model to be implemented will be prepared to develop new programs with confidence and make the needed transitions in order to implement the new vision for school counseling. As programs are developed, implemented, and evaluated, necessary changes will be identified through effective use of data resulting in support for further development. Program evaluations are ongoing models of change. Yet, novice counselors with the new vision will benefit from additional support and knowledge of the change process.

Awareness of the classic difficulty of change in educational systems can be helpful. For many years, education reform efforts have attempted to change education policy (Crissman, Spires, Pope, & Beal, 2000). Gaining knowledge of the history of the change process in general, and in the field of education specifically, can help new counselors understand resistance to change as normal and prepare them to overcome the expected challenges in transforming the role of the school counselor.

Crissman et al. (2000) reported that most educators agree that a passionate shared vision of what a school can become is an important step toward creating a climate of change. Visioning and community building are necessary skills for the counselor who hopes to implement a new model for school counseling. When a school counselor leads a school and its community in the development of a commitment to a mission of high academic achievement for all students while advocating for the removal of barriers to its attainment, a spirit of unity will evolve. The successful induction of a new counselor and the implementation of a newly transformed program can begin to happen in such a climate. Refreshing these skills of visioning and community building as part of the internship experience in an actual school setting and as professional development for the practicing counselor can facilitate the induction process.

In addition to an understanding of the change process, and a working knowledge of procedures for facilitating change (i.e., visioning, mission-building, needs assessment, program development, and evaluation) novice counselors will benefit from continued encouragement from program professors. Sometimes just the right support for a new counselor consists of being reminded that initiating a good idea, finding others who share the vision, and having persistence to achieve the mission will eventually lead to making a difference.

Continuing Professional Development

After CITs become graduates, TSCI programs continue induction through sustained support and professional development emphasizing the importance of professional identity. Encouraging membership in the various professional organizations during and after training helps establish a strong identity in the profession. Additionally, fostering involvement in professional organizations, while in training and as new counselors, is important. Helping CITs and novice counselors attend and present at professional meetings, and working cooperatively with students to conduct research and publish is often a part of the induction processes of many doctoral programs (Boes, Ullery, Millner, & Cobia, 1999). It is likewise important at the master's level for transformed school counselors.

Further emphasis must be placed on providing seminars, retreats, and other staff development opportunities for administrators, teachers, and counselors already on the job, including the novice counselors.

Induction into the profession is the pivotal point on which the development of transformed school counseling programs is positioned. Without support, supervision, and motivation to become lifelong learners, without taking charge of their own growth and continued development of a viable professional identity, the newly transformed school counselor may not continue to grow to meet the changing needs of the complex world in the 21st century.

References

Boes, S.R., Ullery, E.K., Millner, V.S., & Cobia, D.C. (1999). Meeting the challenges of completing a counseling doctoral program. *Journal of Humanistic Education and Development, 37,* 130-144.

Borders, L.D., & Leddick, G.R. (1987). *Handbook of counselor supervision.* Alexandria, VA: American Association for Counseling and Development.

Borders, L.D., & Usher, C.H. (1992). Post-degree supervision: Existing and preferred practices. *Journal of Counseling and Development, 70,* 594-599.

Boyd, J.D., & Walter, P.B. (1975). The school counselor, the cactus, and supervision. *The School Counselor, 23,* 103-107.

Bradley, C., & Fiorini, J. (1999). Evaluation of counseling practicum: National study of programs accredited by CACREP. *Counselor Education & Supervision, 39,* 110-120.

Brott, P.E., & Myers, J.E. (1999). Development of professional school counselor identity: A grounded theory. *Professional School Counseling, 2,* 339-348.

Campbell, C., & Dahir, C. (1997). *Sharing the vision: The national standards for school counseling programs.* Alexandria, VA: American School Counselor Association.

Council for Accreditation of Counseling and Related Educational Programs. (2001). *CACREP Accreditation Manual.* Alexandria, VA: Author.

Crissman, C., Spires, H.A., Pope, C.A., & Beal, C. (2000). Creating pathways of change: One school begins the journey. *Urban Education, 1,* 104-120.

Dahir, C.A. (2000). The national standards for school counseling programs: A partnership in preparing students for the new millennium. *NASSP Bulletin, 84*(616), 68-75.

Education Trust, The. (1997). *The national initiative for transforming school counseling.* Washington: DC: Author. Retrieved January 25, 1998, from http://www.edtrust.org/main/main/school_counseling.asp#website

Gysbers, N.C., & Henderson, P. (1994). *Developing and managing your school guidance program* (2nd ed.). Alexandria, VA: The American Counseling Association.

Hall, D.T. (1987). Careers and socialization. *Journal of Management, 13,* 301-321.

Henderson, P., & Lampe, R.E. (1992). Clinical supervision of school counselors. *The School Counselor, 39,* 151-157.

House, R.M., & Martin, P.J. (1998). Advocating for better futures for all students: A new vision for school counselors. *Education, 119,* 284-291.

Jackson, C.M., Snow, B.M., Phillips, P.L., Boes, S.R., & Rolle, G.E. (1999). Professional school counseling: A new vision at State University of West Georgia. *Georgia School Counselors Association Journal, 1,* 46-51.

Jackson, C.M., Stanard, R.P., Boes, S.R., Painter, L.C., Wulff, M.B., & Rolle, G.E. (2001). The school counselor: A leader in school and community collaboration. *Alabama Counseling Association Journal, 27,* 1-11.

Johnson, L.S. (2000). Promoting professional identity in an era of educational reform. *Professional School Counseling, 4,* 31-41.

Kaplan, L.S., & Evans, M.W. (1999). Hiring the best school counseling candidates to promote students' achievement. *NASSP Bulletin, 83*(603), 34-39.

Matthes, W.A. (1992). Induction of counselors into the profession. *The School Counselor, 39,* 245-250.

Munger, P.F., Myers, R., & Brown, D.F. (1963). Guidance institutes and persistence of attitudes. *The Personnel and Guidance Journal, 41,* 415-419.

Muro, J.J., & Kottman, T. (1995). *Guidance and counseling in the elementary and middle schools.* Madison, WI: Brown & Benchmark.

Myrick, R.D. (1993). *Developmental guidance and counseling: A practical approach* (2nd ed.). Minneapolis, MN: Educational Media.

Nelson, M.D., & Johnson, P. (1999). School counselors as supervisors: An integrated approach for supervising school counseling interns. *Counselor Education & Supervision, 39,* 89-101.

Niebuhr, K.E., Niebuhr, R.E., & Cleveland, W.T. (1999). Principal and counselor collaboration. *Education, 119,* 674-678.

Peace, S.D., & Sprinthall, N.A. (1998). Training school counselors to supervise beginning counselors: Theory, research, and practice. *Professional School Counseling, 1,* 2-8.

Perusse, R., Goodnough, G.E., & Noel, C.J. (2001). A national survey of school counselor preparation programs: Screening methods, faculty experiences, curricular content, and fieldwork requirements. *Counselor Education & Supervision, 40,* 252-262.

Roberts, W.B. (2001). Site supervisors of professional school counseling interns: Suggested guidelines. *Professional School Counseling, 4,* 208-216.

Roberts, E.B., & Borders, L.D. (1994). Supervision of school counselors: Administrative program, and counseling. *The School Counselor, 38,* 86-94.

Schmidt, J.J., & Barret, R.L. (1983). Who's in charge? School counseling supervision in North Carolina. *Counselor Education and Supervision, 23,* 109-116.

Shoffner, M.F., & Briggs, M.K. (2001). An interactive approach for developing interprofessional collaboration: Preparing school counselors. *Counselor Education and Supervision, 40,* 193-202.

Shoffner, M.F., & Williamson, R.D. (2000). Engaging preservice school counselors and principals in dialogue and collaboration. *Counselor Education and Supervision, 40,* 128-140.

Snow, B.M. (2000, February). Professional school counseling at the State University of West Georgia. *Beacon,* 26.

Sutton, J.M., Jr., & Page, B.J. (1994). Post-degree clinical supervision of school counselors. *The School Counselor, 42,* 32-39.

VanZandt, C.E., & Perry, N.S. (1992). Helping the rookie school counselor. A mentoring project. *The School Counselor, 39,* 158-163.

Vaught, C.C. (1995). A letter from a middle school counselor to her principal. *NASSP Bulletin, 79*(565), 20-23.

Watts, R. (1987). Development of professional identity in Black clinical psychology students. *Professional Psychology: Research and Practice, 18,* 28-35.

Wilson, N.S., & Remley, T.P., Jr. (1987). Leadership in guidance: A survey of school counseling supervisors. *Counselor Education and Supervision, 26,* 213-220.

Sue Musheno
Mary Talbert

The Transformed School Counselor in Action

SCHOOL COUNSELORS CONFRONT many different challenges every day. Some challenges are student-related, such as chronic absenteeism, family violence and child abuse, conflicting values between home and school, angry and disruptive students, substance abuse, and underachieving students. Staff-related challenges include working with teachers who may not believe all children can learn, staff who are experiencing high levels of stress in situations they view as overwhelming, or principals who do not know how to best utilize their counselors' skills and instead use them as disciplinarians, substitute teachers, or administrative assistants. Counselors also face challenges that include trying to involve parents in their children's learning, or locating adequate community resources to help students and their families. Finally, counselors working in large urban school systems often fight stifling bureaucracies or red tape.

The number of students who come to school with social or emotional problems has increased over the last decade. Counselors could spend their time counseling these children, but this would allow them to see only 30-35 students a week. Some school counselors do carry a caseload of students with serious problems and often see the same students repeatedly. Yet counselors were not placed in schools to provide counseling services to only a handful of students. When the number of school counselors increased in the 1950s, the expectation was that counselors would work with all students, not just a few. Certainly counselors need to provide individual counseling to some students, but they must refer those with more serious problems to agencies within their surrounding communities. And as pointed out previously in this issue of *TIP*, the mental health model of school counseling has not been effective in increasing students' academic achievement.

Frequently, teachers do not see school counselors as relevant to the school's mission. To be effective in their schools, counselors need to (a) team and consult with teachers to improve student achievement; (b) provide in-service for teachers on children's developmental needs; (c) create mentoring and peer counseling programs to provide support for all students; (d) assess barriers to student learning; (e) collect and interpret student data for use in helping educators engage in needed reforms; (f) advocate for rigorous academic preparation and experiences that will broaden all students' educational and career options; and (g) link with agencies in their communities to provide the widest range of resources for students and their families. The skills counselors need to be effective include teaming and collaboration, leadership, assessment and use of data to bring about change, advocacy,

Sue Musheno and Mary Talbert are counselors with the Columbus, Ohio, public school system.

and counseling and coordination (Education Trust, 1997).

The Transforming School Counseling Initiative (TSCI) has focused on developing the five skills listed above. The six TSCI counselor education programs have strived to prepare prospective counselors who will be able to use these skills to make a difference in the schools in which they are hired. A series of scenarios demonstrating how transformed school counselors would function using these skills follows.

Scenario 1: Teaming and collaboration (with other educators)

Beth Hardy, the school counselor at Brown Elementary, a large urban elementary school, arrives early to prepare for an Intervention Assistance Team meeting (IAT) scheduled for 7:45 a.m. The meeting will focus on generating strategies to help a student, John, improve his academic achievement. Other educators, such as John's teacher, the school nurse, the reading teacher, the school psychologist (in certain situations), and a counselor from a local mental health agency join Beth. When Beth started counseling at Brown, no structure for staffing students with achievement or behavior problems existed. Teachers referred students to her, but there was no systematic discussion of children's problems. Beth found herself trying to track down teachers individually, often at recess, just to talk to them about the student they had referred. These conversations were brief and didn't give the teacher and counselor time to collaborate on possible strategies for improving the situation for which the student was referred. Feeling frustrated about the lack of coherent interventions to help children, Beth talked to the school principal about starting Intervention Assistance Teams. Beth believed that bringing together the student's teacher and other members of the student services team would help them understand all aspects of a student's situation as they tried to generate an action plan to deal with whatever issues were involved.

After only a few weeks, the IAT approach was widely accepted by the teachers as they began to see the benefits of more planned interventions. They were trying out new strategies in the classroom that they had learned from other members of the IAT. They also reported that they felt more support in dealing with classroom-related problems.

Scenario 2: Teaming and collaboration (with the community)

Involving the counselor from a local social agency in the meetings was Beth's idea, too. She convinced the principal that the school needed to link more effectively with community resources. As a representative of the school, Beth visited a local mental health center and asked the director about the possibility of the two agencies working together to serve both the students and their families. The director was receptive and had the resources to assign one of his counselors to the school for 15 hours a week. Beth, serving in her role as coordinator of mental health services in the school, meets with the agency counselor an hour each week to discuss the students with whom the agency counselor is working. One of the major benefits of this collaboration is that families of some of the children have also received assistance. The agency counselor has made home visits and has linked some of the parents to other forms of assistance in the community, such as a food pantry, a job-retraining agency, and a local church that is providing after-school tutoring for children. The extra help with students whose problems are quite serious is also welcome. The agency counselor is conducting small-group meetings with students who get into fights easily and students whose parents have recently divorced. Many of these students have so much stress in their lives that they have been unable to succeed in school. The goal of the small-group sessions is to help students gain the skills to better manage their anger or the stress of major changes at home.

Scenario 3: Leadership

Sue is a middle school counselor in a large urban district. She is assigned to two schools, serving 450 students and 25 faculty in one building and 535 students and 30 faculty in the other. Sue has been a school counselor for more than a decade. Her colleagues consider her to be one of the leaders in her district because she has previously assumed leadership positions in her local counseling association and on staff development committees in the school district. Three years ago, Sue read an article about the new American School Counselor Association (ASCA) national standards indicating what students should know and be able to do as a result of participating in a school counseling program. Realizing that her district's program was out-of-date, Sue contacted her director of guidance to inquire when the district's school counseling program was due for revision. The director indicated that it was actually time to revise it and asked Sue to assume a leadership role in this effort.

Sue has seen the impact of standards-driven educational reform in her district as well as the way teachers are being held accountable for student learning. She realized that counselors needed to reexamine their mission and the models they have used in the past. The members of the committee revising the counseling program held numerous discussions about the need to move away from a mental health model toward a more activist model in which counselors collaborate with the community to bring resources into the school and to families. They also discussed the importance of counselors working more closely with teachers to help students acquire learning and study skills.

Sue and the director of guidance contacted a counselor educator from a nearby university to work with the committee as they rethought their program and organized it around the ASCA national standards. The counselor educator encouraged the counselors on the revision committee to gather data about student performance throughout the district, and to look at a recent evaluation of the school district before deciding the standards on which to base the program. The counselors spent time collecting the data and reviewing the evaluation study. They were particularly alarmed with the students' low proficiency test scores. They knew their revised program needed to show other educators that counselors were committed to helping students improve academically. They discussed the importance of encouraging students to take rigorous courses so they would be prepared to pass the proficiency tests and ready to pursue postsecondary educational options. Some counselors were very concerned about the serious mental and emotional problems of their students. Sue pointed to the many community resources that needed to be tapped and reported that some agencies were even willing to write grants to help bring in more resources. She reminded everyone that each counselor served more than 400 students, and if they dealt with only the 25 or 30 students with the most serious problems, others would not see them as fulfilling the mission of their program. The high school counselors claimed their principals expected them to do too much clerical work. Others felt they were being used as assistant principals. The director of guidance told the committee that once the school board approved the new counseling program, the counselors would be accountable for delivering it.

The committee reviewed the ASCA standards and developed student competencies on which to focus. It took 1½ years from the time the committee began until it completed its work. The program includes a clear mission statement focusing on the school counselor's role in supporting student learning and achievement. To facilitate the implementation of the program, a committee of counselors wrote a detailed classroom curriculum guide so the counselors could reach every student at some time during the year.

Scenario 4: Assessing and using data

Sherwood Middle School is located in a suburban neighborhood and enjoys a stellar academic reputation. The principal wants to gain recognition as one of the outstanding schools in his state but can't achieve that recognition because of the attendance figures. He has charged the school counselor, Orlando Jones, with improving the average daily attendance at the school. In fact, the principal has charged the entire school staff to develop plans for improving student attendance. He has let Orlando know that he expects him to lead this effort.

Orlando reviews what the school already has tried. He remembers the approach they tried last year in which teachers set up an incentive plan for their classrooms. Weekly improvement figures were placed outside the door of each classroom, and students were encouraged to come to school and urge their peers to do so, too. Homerooms showing improvement were rewarded with pizza parties or movies. However, after a few weeks in which attendance increased, progress slowed and absences returned to their previously high rates. Orlando concluded that he might not fully understand the nature of the attendance problem and would benefit from analyzing the attendance data. Working with the attendance secretary, Orlando disaggregated the data to determine who was missing, where they lived, their grade level, and their level of achievement. He discovered that 20 students were responsible for more than 50% of the days missed. Orlando spent part of three days gathering information about the 20 students so he had a complete picture of the each individual student's situation.

Next, Orlando presented the list of students to the staff and explained how he had arrived at his findings. Teachers who had these students in their classes agreed to meet with the counselor over lunch the next day to learn more about them and to discuss what they might do to increase attendance. At lunch, Orlando discussed the students' achievement levels and profiled a few of the students who were facing difficult challenges at home. He was careful not to impinge on the students' or their families' privacy but was able to help teachers understand the special circumstances that some faced. Orlando also wanted to make certain the teachers understood that if these 20 students attended school three more days each month, the school's average daily attendance would improve by one point. Successfully intervening with 20 students could not only help them achieve academically but could result in school improvement in terms of attendance. Orlando described how he had contacted the county juvenile justice department and the public health department to see what resources were available to assist the school. He discovered that the county juvenile justice department had special funding for school-based programs and would provide personnel to conduct home visits with the parents of these 20 students since some of them had already had brushes with the law. After a second meeting with the teachers, Orlando was able to convince them to work in teams of two to mentor each student. These mentoring teams agreed to provide support and encouragement to students with the goal of helping them realize the school cared and wanted them to learn.

The teachers' concern and response to these 20 students resulted in others becoming interested in the mentoring program. Teachers reported that they enjoyed the more personal time spent with the students, and others on the staff became mentors also. Students experiencing other challenges in their lives (e.g., an alcoholic parent, recent death or illness in the family) were identified and linked with interested teachers. Because Orlando continued to monitor the attendance data, he was able to demonstrate that average daily attendance improved. Within six months, Orlando had established himself as creative problem solver.

Scenario 5: Advocacy

Jodi Freeman is a high school counselor at Martin Luther King High School. King is located in a deteriorating neighborhood in a large Midwestern city. Jodi is the junior and senior counselor, and this is her second year at the school. When Jodi started at King, she was concerned about the situation she faced. The senior class was comprised of 88 students, most of whom had not done any educational or career planning to prepare for the future. The good news was that two years ago the school had aligned its curriculum with state standards, and students had been encouraged to take more rigorous courses. Many of the students seemed willing to listen to Jodi as she talked about two- and four-year college options. She was worried that the academic records of many of the students were average or below average but did not let that stop her from encouraging them to sign up for the SAT. Jodi convinced some teachers to help students prepare for the SAT, and the principal located extra money in the district to pay them for their time. Jodi talked to a few college representatives who were interested in recruiting minority students and became convinced that she might help students get college scholarships.

Armed with confidence in herself and a belief that, with support, these students could succeed in college, Jodi collected information, including applications, from 35-40 colleges that offered scholarships to minority students. Working with students in small groups, she helped them complete their applications. She held information meetings for parents in the evenings and on Saturdays. Volunteers from local colleges visited the school to discuss financial aid options. She took students to visit colleges and held conference calls with recruiters from colleges too far away to visit. Some of the more academically oriented students were accepted to the schools they wanted in December of that year. As the news that students were being admitted and were receiving scholarships became public, other students were motivated to complete their applications.

The senior English teachers decided to support Jodi's effort by reminding and encouraging the students to complete the necessary forms as well as offering to proofread their essays or biographical statements. The atmosphere of the school began to change. Parents began to stop by to meet the counselor and let her know that they supported her. By May, 56 students had been offered college scholarships. The staff and parents were amazed. Jodi, who was also surprised, resolved to begin planning for the next year. She knew that next year could be even more successful.

Scenario 6: Counseling and coordination

Mary is an elementary school counselor who works in a district similar to Sue's. In fact, counselors in her district developed a school counseling program using the ASCA standards last year. She is in her first month of school and has been trying to arrange her daily schedule to reflect the new counseling program. An example of Mary's typical day follows:

- 8:15 Teacher consultation
- 8:25 Check schedule for the day
- 8:30 Intervention Assistance Team meeting
- 9:00 Planning and organizing material for individual and group sessions
- 9:15 Classroom Guidance, 3rd grade
- 9:45 Individual Counseling #1
- 10:05 Individual Counseling #2
- 10:25 Meeting with principal to discuss teacher in-service
- 10:40 Phone conference with parent
- 11:00 Classroom Guidance, 3rd grade
- 11:30 Lunch
- 12:00 Student Council
- 12:30 Career Day – planning meeting with volunteers
- 1:00 Classroom Guidance, 3rd grade
- 1:35 Individual counseling #3
- 2:00 Peacemaker's Group, 1st grade
- 2:30 Recess (observe student who has been referred)
- 2:45 Classroom Guidance, 3rd grade
- 3:15 Phone call with social agency counselor
- 3:50 30-minute in-service for teachers on test interpretation
- 4:30 Review day and document activities
- 5:15 Leave school for home

Mary knows from experience that someone always needs to talk or to seek advice, so she has built the time into the daily schedule. She has set aside time each day to be available to any teachers who wish to talk before class. This morning she is planning to meet with the teacher of the student she expects to see at 9:45 a.m. After that, she will check her daily and weekly schedules. An Intervention Assistance Team meeting is her first scheduled meeting. This is a problem-solving group that includes the building administrator, teachers, parents, a psychologist, a community liaison, and the school counselor. The purpose of the meeting is to brainstorm strategies to help the child be successful at school.

Having previously arranged a classroom guidance schedule, Mary will conduct three 30-minute classroom lessons in the third grade. The lesson focuses on building skills to help students achieve, which is found in the guidance curriculum that is a part of the district's school counseling program. Counselors throughout the district follow the same classroom guidance curriculum schedule to ensure that all students will have equal opportunity to work with the counselor. The elementary classroom guidance schedule in Mary's district features a different theme each month:

Month	Grade	Theme
September	K-5	Introduction of Counselors
October	3	Success for Academic Achievement
November	1	Social Skills
December	K	All About Me
January	5	Conflict Resolution
February	2	Career Choices
May	4	Decision Making
May	5	Transition to Middle School

Classroom guidance allows Mary to work with every student in a developmental and proactive manner. Last year she worked with each of the 360 students at least twice during the school year.

Small-group counseling also constitutes a significant part of her day. To determine the types of small group sessions to conduct, Mary analyzed school data for attendance, achievement, and the behavioral concerns teachers reported and then made a list of possible group topics. She asked teachers to rank the topics on the list and two needs emerged: (a) groups to increase academic achievement and (b) groups to help students improve their behavior (e.g., anger management, conflict resolution). Mary developed small-group activities around these topics and named one "the Winner's Group," for intermediate students who needed skills to increase their achievement and reduce off-task classroom behavior, and the other "the Peacemaker's Group," to help primary students learn conflict resolution and anger management skills.

In her weekly Winner's Group, Mary creates activities using the efficacy ideas below to help students learn how to control their thoughts and their behavior:

Efficacy Idea 1: Smart is not something you *are*; smart is something you get.
Efficacy Idea 2: Our thoughts affect how we behave.
Efficacy Idea 3: If you think you can and work hard, you will get smart.
Efficacy Idea 4: Feelings affect our thoughts and our behavior.
Efficacy Idea 5: Setting goals helps us achieve!
Efficacy Idea 6: We can use the support of our family and friends to be successful students.
Efficacy Idea 7: Affirmations are positive self-talk. They can help us achieve our goals.
Efficacy Idea 8: My behavior has a direct relationship to my school success.

Typically, the small groups consist of 4-6 students who meet once a week for 6-8 weeks. These groups constitute a significant departure from the ones Mary had previously conducted, such as groups for children experiencing grief or children of divorce and remarriage. She still runs a group for children of divorce, however, many of the mental health-related groups are now conducted by a social agency counselor who has been assigned to her school. Mary and the agency counselor meet each week to discuss the progress of his groups. She also, with the help of teachers, identifies students who could benefit from small-group counseling. Mary met with an average of 12 groups during the past school year, and her colleague from the local mental health center conducted 10 sessions. They then worked together to evaluate the impact of their groups. Student questionnaires, rating scales that teachers complete regarding student behavior, student discipline data, and grade point averages are all used to determine if the small-group counseling is effective.

Conclusion

This article has described the five skills the Transforming School Counseling Initiative believes will equip today's school counselors to become leaders in educational reform and advocates for improving students' academic achievement. Scenarios have shown how counselors can put these skills into practice.

References

Education Trust, The. (1997). *The national guidance and counseling reform program.* Washington, DC: Author.

Peggy LaTurno Hines

Transforming the Rural¹ School Counselor

NEARLY 27% OF AMERICAN school children attend schools in rural areas or small towns. Forty percent of all teachers are employed in rural locales, which contain almost half of the country's public elementary and secondary schools and 60% of the public school districts. Yet, only 22% of the total dollars spent on education in the United States goes to rural schools (National Center for Education Statistics, 1998b, 1998c, 1998d, 1999d; National Education Association [NEA], 1998; United States Government Accounting Office [USAO], 1996).

While much attention has appropriately been paid to the needs and issues facing urban education (Beeson & Strange, 2000; Sherwood, 2001), little research, debate, or funding has focused on the differences between urban and rural education or the specific needs and issues impacting rural education. In fact, rural education has been called the "orphaned stepchild of the national education research program" (Sherwood, 2001, p. 1).

Even less attention has been paid to the role of rural school counselors (Morrissette, 1997, 2000). Not only do rural school counselors face the same problems as their urban peers but they must work with additional characteristics unique to the rural environment. While rural school counselors have been neglected in the literature, some would argue they have also been underutilized in their schools. The

Peggy LaTurno Hines is an associate professor of education at Indiana State University.

Education Trust (1997) maintained that rural school counselors are not a part of the educational reform that has been sweeping the United States during the last two decades. Staff at the Trust suggested that school counseling and school counselors must be transformed if they wish to be integral to the mission of schools. This article describes the underlying knowledge, skills, and attitudes that transformed school counselors need in order to work effectively in rural schools and communities. It then provides a snapshot of the salient issues facing rural education and communities, and examples of how transformed school counselors might positively impact these issues.

Transforming School Counseling

The Transforming School Counseling Initiative (TSCI) is grounded in the belief that school counselors can and must be facilitators of the change needed to remove the systemic barriers that keep all children from achieving academic success. The knowledge and skills these professional counselors possess are vital to any effort to raise student achievement.

The Education Trust identified seven areas in which the transformed school counselor must be proficient: leadership, advocacy, using data to spur change, counseling and coordination, teaming and collaboration, multicultural and diversity competencies, and technology. School counselors, when effectively employing these skills through an understanding of the specific context, strengths, and needs of rural schools and communities, can have a dynamic impact on students, their families, the school, and the rural community as a whole.

The Transformed Rural School Counselor

How do transformed school counselors bring together the knowledge and skills of the TSCI with the rural community context and strengths? First, they must have a keen understanding and genuine appreciation for the communities in which they work. Haas and Lambert (1995) argued that working in rural schools and communities

> requires belief in the strength of places and cultures that have usually been identified by their putative weaknesses: rurality, poverty, and various background characteristics (ethnicity, gender, or age). In the dynamic of mutual respect and collaboration, a fresh eye is cast on rural communities. Long-standing needs become opportunities for collaboration and learning. Resources are uncovered, redefined, and invested in new ways. Powerful academic potential is discovered in the very qualities—often dismissed by outsiders—that rural people have always valued in their schools: their capacity to support social relationships, to anchor community life, to keep students close to home and rooted in the culture, and to give identity to communities. (p. 141)

From this understanding and appreciation for the strength inherent in rural diversity, the school counselor must be prepared to lead the way toward the development of a culturally responsive school and community (Lee, 2001). Lee admonishes counselors to be "agents of change with the knowledge and skill to translate cultural awareness into constructive action" (p. 258). Equity, access, and educational justice issues—be it within subgroups of the rural community itself or between rural and urban differences—must become a priority if other issues such as rural student achievement, poverty, and homelessness ever hope to be effectively addressed.

Rural school counselors must be willing and ready to be leaders and apologists of effective advocacy strategies. These strategies must revolve around people and relationships (Hurley, 1999). As described above, the backbone of rural life is personal and communal relationships. Yet, most rural education reform efforts tend to leave rural residents out of educational decision making (Howley & Howley, 1995; Sher, 1995; Theobald & Nachtigal, 1995). Smith (1999) posits that any intervention, strategy, program or activity will be more powerful when it is student- and community-centered. Rural school counselors need to create the norm of inclusiveness that values the input of those groups (e.g., parents, students, the poor, and dropouts) that are usually marginalized in educational reform and community development endeavors (Haas & Lambert, 1995). To truly engage this wide range of diversity is to tap into the power inherent within the rural community. Yet, to do this takes consistent, meaningful, two-way communication and a deep respect for the diversity of cultural history and values.

It also takes the development of a common vision of success for every student. Rural school counselors can facilitate the development of a school/community vision of student success. Theobald and Mills (1995) argue that schools must rediscover the importance of community and caring. The creation of a vision bonds a school and community together, provides a common direction, fosters cohesiveness and commitment to growth and change, creates energy for change, and rekindles the hope of a bright future for the community (Reynolds & Hines, 2001). This vision then becomes the basis for the school and community's goals and strategies.

While vision provides the direction, it is data that provide a sense of urgency for change by showing a current picture of the rural school and community. When this picture is compared to the vision, tension is created, which, in turn, creates an imperative for change. Transformed rural school counselors know how to collect, analyze, and present data to spur change. While examples of the use of data are mentioned below, the importance of disaggregated data cannot be stressed enough. Disaggregated data help ensure that groups of students who may not be achieving as well aren't lost in the aggregate summary data (Reynolds & Hines, 2001). It is when goals are school and community vision-based and data-driven that change can become systemic. Yet, this type of change does not occur overnight. It is hard work that takes patience and persistence.

As goals and strategies are developed, school counselors must be aware of the rural context of scarcity. "Rural communities suffer from a shortage of resources, a lack of service coordination, and restrictions of categorical funding streams" (Dunbar, 1999, p. 15). Part of the role of TSCI counselors is teaming and collaboration. Rural school counselors must be creative as they design structures to work toward goals. Facilitating the formation of agency, organization, and/or business collaboratives is one strategy. Community collaboratives can explore the possibility of service integration (e.g., wraparound services) and various models of blended funding (Dunbar, 1999).

Finally, transformed rural school counselors must continuously work to build social capital. Coleman (as sited in Miller, 1995) sees social capital as those resources contained within the rural social fabric, such as interpersonal relationships, values, and social networks, that can positively impact personal and social growth. This social capital then becomes the source of energy needed to sustain movement toward the school and community vision.

Rural School and Community Issues and the Transformed School Counselor

While rural schools and communities face the same problems as do urban locales, rural areas must face additional, often complicating, problems. Major issues facing rural schools and communities are briefly reviewed below, and examples of transformed rural school counselor interventions are shared. It is important to note that the examples given are sample ideas. For systemic change to occur, interventions and strategies should be designed based on the paradigm just described.

Rural student achievement

Gibbs (2000) reported that the most recent studies find the academic performance of rural and urban students to be comparable; however, when the National Assessment of Educational Progress (NAEP) scores are disaggregated into urban, suburban, and rural scores, areas for continued attention emerge. While rural students consistently scored at about the same level as or above urban students in math, reading, and writing, they consistently scored lower than their suburban cohorts in the same areas (NCES, 1996a, 1996b, 1996c, 1998e, 1998f, 1998g, 1998h, 1998i, 1998j).

Although rural schools have improved their high school graduation rates, nonmetropolitan students drop out of school at a higher rate (12.7%) than metropolitan students (11.6%) (Sherman, 1992; United States Department of Commerce, 1998), and those rural students who left high school returned to complete high school or earn a GED at lower rates than their urban peers (Perroncel, 2000). In general, rural students have lower career aspirations, and fewer graduates prepare for and enroll in postsecondary education (Gibbs, 2000; Perroncel, 2000). While those who do enroll in some type of postsecondary education perform as well as their urban cohorts, only 54% of rural students apply to college, compared with 62% of their suburban peers (Stern, 1994).

Transformed rural school counselors need to be leaders in helping the school and community understand student achievement data. Counselors can also facilitate the collection of disaggregated achievement-related data to look at issues educational research has shown impacts student achievement (e.g., attendance, teacher use of hands-on learning activities and authentic assessment, discipline referrals, parent involvement, homelessness, and poverty). Through the use of data, the rural school counselor can become a powerful advocate for additional academic support programs for students, faculty professional development, community outreach and program development.

School operation issues

In addition to the normal funding challenges generally impacting education, rural schools face a number of additional funding challenges. Rural schools, which account for almost 50% of U.S. public school buildings and employ 40% of the teachers to educate 27% of the school children, receive only 22% of the dollars spent on education. Even though rural residents pay a greater percentage of their income on education, schools face lower revenues from a smaller local tax base due to lower per capita income and less business and industry (Perroncel, 2000). Thus, rural schools have less to spend per student than do urban schools. An issue bound to further complicate the school funding problem is that enrollment in rural schools is projected to grow by 1.3 million students in the next few years (Synder, Hoffman, & Geddes, 1999).

Most rural schools are also faced with higher operational costs. The cost of many services, such as special education, is greater for small school districts because costs are being spread out over fewer students. Also, rural school districts must spend more per-pupil on transportation than their urban cohorts. These increased costs lead to rural school systems providing fewer programs and services, such as alternative schools, vocational programs, a wide variety of high school classes, extended day programs, and programs for special needs students (Dewees, 1999; NEA, 1998; Perroncel, 2000; Sherman, 1992).

Another issue that impacts the operational costs of rural schools is the overall poor condition of school facilities. Rural school buildings are, on average, older than suburban schools and about the same age as urban schools (NCES, 2000a). Older buildings are less energy-efficient, and thus cost more to maintain. Also, many rural schools report struggling to meet federal mandates concerning the removal of hazardous building materials (e.g., asbestos) and the installation of features (e.g., access ramps) required by the Americans with Disabilities Act of 1990 (Dewees, 1999).

Rural school counselors must be advocates for their students, schools, and communities at the local, state, and national levels. The inequity in funding for rural school districts is a major issue. School counselors need to be activists who bring together rural educators and citizens to help legislators understand rural funding dilemmas and change school funding formulas.

Counselors in rural schools can use their skills in technology to help them stay abreast of state and national legislation. The Internet provides a plethora of information on external funding opportunities that may be used for program development and implementation or capital expenditures.

Faculty issues

Rural schools are experiencing teacher and administrator shortages (Beeson & Strange, 2000; Collins, 1999; Gibbs, 2000). This is partially due to lower salaries. The average base salary for rural teachers ($33,829) is $4,000 less than central city teachers and more than $8,000 below urban fringe faculty (NCES, 1998a). Not only is recruitment difficult but so is the retention of rural staff (Beeson & Strange, 2000). Rural faculty tend to be younger, less educated, and slightly less experienced than their urban peers (Gibbs, 2000; Kannapel & DeYoung, 1999; NCES, 1999e). Rural educators are also less likely than central city and urban fringe educators to have participated in a formal induction program when they first began to teach (U.S. Department of Education, 1999e).

Rural students generally rate their teachers as high or higher than their urban and suburban peers (Metropolitan Life & Louis Harris Associates, Inc., 1997a, 1997b), and rural teachers have reported greater satisfaction with their work environment and more active participation in their local communities than their urban peers (Gibbs, 2000). At the same time, they have also reported that they feel socially, culturally, and professionally isolated (Collins, 1999).

Rural school counselors can have a tremendous impact on the faculty. The degree to which faculty become involved in the rural community has been shown to influence their decision to remain (Collins, 1999). As they establish relationships with faculty, school counselors can encourage involvement in local activities in which teachers show an interest, and can facilitate the development of school programs for students that revolve around faculty avocations, such as a drama club for a teacher who was a college thespian.

More importantly, school counselors can collaborate individually with teachers or assist in the creation of faculty professional development study groups that focus on the development and implementation of new instructional strategies. For example, a group could be formed to develop lesson plans based on the eight learning characteristics of rural students identified by Potterfield and Pace (as cited in Fitzgerald & Bloodsworth, 1996). Additionally, school counselors can work with administrators to develop meaningful mentoring programs not just for teachers new to the profession but also for those new to teaching in rural locales. Mentoring groups can provide the social support new teachers need to relieve their stress.

Parental involvement

Rural parents have reported their involvement in school activities at about the same rate as urban parents (NCES, 1999b, 1999c). They also reported being less satisfied with their child's school and teachers, academic standards, and order and discipline (NCES, 2000c).

One of the inherent strengths in rural schools is a strong sense of community. Parents, for the most part, are ready and willing to be involved in their child's education. A perceived lack of involvement may have nothing to do with the parents' desire to be involved. Local employers, due to the nature of cooperative job tasks, may simply be unable to let their employees take time off during the day to come to a school conference or take a phone call from a teacher. Parents may need information and training on how to participate in the educational process, or they may feel unwelcome at school due to their own negative association with the school and educational environment (Campbell, 1993; Chavkin & Williams, 1989). Transformed school counselors, through their understanding of the unique context within the rural community, can facilitate the development of strategies that reach out to parents instead of expecting parents to come to the school.

Poverty

Rural America is significantly poorer than metropolitan areas as a whole and nearly as poor as central cities. Of the 250 poorest counties in America, 244 are rural (Beeson & Strange, 2000). In 1999, the rural household poverty rate was 16%, compared with 13% in metropolitan counties. An additional 26% of rural residents lived just above the poverty line, compared to 18% of urban dwellers (Huang, 1999). Rural African Americans and Native Americans suffer greater rates of poverty, 35% and 36% respectively, compared with 12% among rural Euramericans (Huang, 1999). Rural children have a higher poverty rate than their urban peers. Dagata (1999) reported on 1996 data that showed 24% of nonmetropolitan children living in poverty compared to 22% of metropolitan children.

Rural homelessness is as prevalent as urban homelessness. Vissing (1996) reported that half of rural homeless households were families with children, and that rural female-headed homeless families were twice as prevalent as their urban counterparts (32% compared to 16%). Later, Vissing (1998) noted the lack of shelters in rural areas and the tendency for the rural homeless to move in temporarily with family or friends. She argued that homelessness is a more difficult challenge for rural educators due to the higher rate of homelessness involving children and the lack of attention paid to the rural context.

School counselors can coordinate counseling interventions that address the needs of students, as well as assist in the development of community agency collaboratives that work together to link community resources, support high-quality and developmentally appropriate programs, and provide a continuity of services. In addition, counselors can facilitate the development of faculty and agency professional development that focuses on the instructional needs of impoverished students, and work with administrators to review policies and guidelines to ensure their appropriateness with respect to homeless children (Vissing, 1998).

Economic issues

Rural economic development is difficult due to the geographic remoteness to urban areas, the lack of adequate transportation systems, and the lack of skilled workers. Jobs created in rural areas tend to be part of the secondary labor market, consisting mainly of jobs that require low levels of education and offer low wages with little or no benefits (Shaffer & Seyfrit, 1999). In fact, in 1996 the rural workforce earned only about four-fifths of what their urban counterparts earned (Huang, 1999). Another factor that influences economic development is that rural communities often find themselves in a brain-drain situation. Students who do well in school and go on to postsecondary training often migrate to urban areas to find the primary labor market's high skill-high pay jobs. This leaves the low-skilled residents, a higher percent of whom are high school dropouts, in the rural job market, making it even more difficult to attract the primary labor business and industry (Herzog & Pittman, 1999; Shaffer & Seyfrit, 1999; Sherman, 1992).

"Small towns and rural areas have been disadvantaged with regard to the availability and accessibility both of human services and of competent professionals to provide those services" (Carlton-LaNey, Edwards, & Reid, 1999, p. 9). Rural areas, while perhaps having lower housing costs, tend to have a higher cost of living due to added transportation costs and the lack of competition. Since a rural economy can support only a few businesses, there is little competition to help keep prices down (Hamilton & Seyfrit, 1993; Perroncel, 2000).

Medical and mental health services are limited in rural areas. Specialists are a rarity, and community services tend to be fragmented. Rural children are less likely to have access to health services and to have health insurance. Furthermore, due to low household income and logistics, rural children may be less likely to receive needed medical attention (Perroncel, 2000; Sherman, 1992).

There is also a lack of easily accessible and affordable telecommunications technology in rural areas. This contributes to the fact that a smaller percentage of rural Americans have computers and Internet connections than their urban counterparts (Byers, 1996). Barriers to access exist due to the increased cost of providing wireless telecommunication services in rural areas where distance and low population density are defining characteristics. Moreover, there is a perceived lack of value of these services. Rural residents are less informed than urbanites as to how information technologies work and can enhance their economic and cultural opportunities. Instead, they believe that information technologies are too costly in both dollars and time to be worth the investment (Byers, 1996).

Transformed rural school counselors can foster partnerships between faculty and community business and industry leaders. These partnerships then work to focus the curriculum on issues of importance to the community and students, and the community can be used as a laboratory for learning (Miller, 1995; Theobald & Nachtigal, 1995). Additionally, school counselors can facilitate the formation of school and community collaboratives focused on the development of accessible and affordable services. These strong linkages between school and community help strengthen and sustain the rural community on numerous levels. Once these linkages are established, they create an infrastructure that is dynamic and available to respond to community needs.

Drug use and violence

According to the Center on Addiction and Substance Abuse (CASA, 2000), rural eighth graders are 104% more likely to use amphetamines than their peers in urban areas, and are 50% more likely to use cocaine. The CASA study also reported rural eighth grade students were 34% likelier than those in urban centers to smoke marijuana, 83% likelier to use crack, 29% likelier to drink alcohol, 70% likelier to have been drunk, nearly five times likelier to use smokeless tobacco, and more than twice as likely to smoke cigarettes. The report states that since 1990, drug law violations increased more in rural communities, and that drugs are as available in rural America as they are in urban locales. At the same time, rural areas are less equipped to deal with the consequences. Drug use has placed enormous pressure on rural hospitals, child welfare systems, treatment facilities, and law enforcement.

With the emergence of gangs, delinquency, and youth drug use, crime levels in rural areas are at historic highs (Donnermeyer, 1995). Rural schools reported fewer criminal incidents and serious discipline issues than their urban counterparts but more than urban fringe schools. In a survey of rural educators, Peterson, Beekley, Speaker, and Pietrzak (1998) found that within the past two years nearly half of the respondents had personally experienced some form of school-related violence at least once. They also reported increases in violence at all school levels that they attributed to violence in the home and a lack of family involvement and supervision.

One of the main difficulties in addressing these issues is the tendency for rural schools and communities to be in a state of denial concerning drug use and violence (Herzog & Pittman, 1999). This may stem from not wanting to believe that known students and families have problems that need to be addressed. Rural school counselors can use data to facilitate the recognition of drug use and violence as a school/community problem. Through collaborative efforts, the school and community can identify the local issues that must be addressed in order to design strategies to provide training, treatment, and resources.

Conclusion

This article has described the salient issues facing rural educators and communities, such as student achievement, the recruitment and retention of faculty, and how economic development influences access and affordability to services. It provides a description of the rural school counselor's role and how counselors must use their knowledge and skills to transform counseling in this setting. Through their understanding of the specific rural context, strengths, and issues, counselors in rural schools can build the social capital needed to address the barriers to academic success for every student.

Note

1. There are numerous definitions of the term *rural*. Unless otherwise noted, this article defines *rural* or *nonmetropolitan* as the combination of two Census Bureau classifications: (a) small town, a place not within a metropolitan statistical area with a population of at least 2,500 but less than 25,000, and (b) a place with a population of less than 2,500. *Urban,* or *metropolitan,* encompasses the five classifications denoted as urban: large central city, mid-size central city, urban fringe of large city, urban fringe of mid-size city, and large town.

References

Beeson, E., & Strange, M. (2000). *Why rural matters: The need for every state to take action on rural education.* Washington, DC: Rural School and Community Trust. Retrieved June 14, 2001, from http://www.ruraledu.org/streport/summary.html.

Byers, A. (1996). Communities address barriers to connectivity [Electronic version]. *Rural clearinghouse digest on rural telecommunications, 3*(1).

Campbell, C. (1993). Strategies for reducing parent resistance to consultation in the schools. *Elementary School Guidance & Counseling, 28,* 83-91.

Carlton-LaNey, I.B., Edwards, R.L., & Reid, P.N. (1999). Small towns and rural communities: From romantic notions to harsh realities. In I.B. Carlton-LaNey, R.L. Edwards, & P.N. Reid (Eds.), *Preserving and strengthening small towns and rural communities* (pp. 5-12). Washington, DC: NASW Press.

Chavkin, N.F., & Williams, D.L. (1989). Low-income parents' attitudes toward parent involvement in education. *Journal of Sociology and Social Welfare, 16*(3), 17-28.

Collins, T. (1999). *Attracting and retaining teachers in rural areas.* ERIC Digest. Charleston, WV: ERIC Clearinghouse on Rural Education and Small Schools. (ERIC Document Reproduction Service No. ED438152). Retrieved June 20, 2001 from http://www.ed.gov/databases/ERIC_Digests/ed438152.html

Dagata, E. (1999). The socioeconomic well-being of rural children lags that of urban children. *Rural Conditions and Trends, 9*(2), 85-90.

Dewees, S. (1999). *Improving rural school facilities for teaching and learning.* ERIC Digest. Charleston, WV: ERIC Clearinghouse on Rural Education and Small Schools. (ERIC Document Reproduction Service No. ED438153). Retrieved June 20, 2001 from http://www.ed.gov/databases/ERIC_Digests/ed438153.html

Donnermeyer, J.F. (1995). *Crime and violence in rural communities.* Columbus, OH: National Rural Crime Prevention Center. Retrieved April 12, 2001, from http://www.ncrel.org/sdrs/areas/issues/envrnmnt/drugfree/v1donner.htm

Dunbar, E.R. (1999). Strengthening services in rural communities through blended funding. In I.B. Carlton-LaNey, R.L. Edwards, & P.N. Reid (Eds.), *Preserving and strengthening small towns and rural communities* (pp. 15-26). Washington, DC: NASW Press.

Education Trust, The. (1997). *Specific counseling skills necessary to transform the role of the school counselor for the 90's and beyond.* Washington, DC: Author. Retrieved June 29, 2001, from http://www.edtrust.org/main/school_counseling.asp#specific

Fitzgerald, D.F., & Bloodsworth, G. (1996). Addressing the neglected needs of rural learnings: A learning style approach. *Clearing House, 69*(3), 169-170.

Gibbs, R. (2000). The challenge ahead for rural schools. *Forum for Applied Research and Public Policy, 15*(1), 82-87.

Hamilton, L.C., & Seyfrit, C.L. (1993). Town-village contrasts in Alaskan youth aspirations. *Artic, 46*(3), 255-263.

Haas, T., & Lambert, R. (1995). To establish the bonds of common purpose and mutual enjoyment. *Phi Delta Kappan, 77*(2), 136-142.

Herzog, M.J., & Pittman, R. (1999). The nature of rural schools: Trends, perceptions and values. In D.M. Chalker (Ed.), *Leadership for rural school: Lessons for all educators* (pp. 11-23). Lancaster, PA: Technomic.

Howley, C.B., & Howley, A. (1995). The power of babble: Technology and rural education. *Phi Delta Kappan, 77*(2), 126-131.

Huang, G.G. (1999). *Sociodemographic changes: Promise and problems for rural education.* ERIC Digest. Charleston, WV: ERIC Clearinghouse on Rural Education and Small Schools. (ERIC Document Reproduction Service No. ED425048). Retrieved June 15, 2001, from http://www.ed.gov/databases/ERIC_Digests/ed425048.html

Hurley, J.C. (1999). Leading rural schools: Building relationships and structures. In D.M. Chalker (Ed.), *Leadership for rural school: Lessons for all educators* (pp. 137-156). Lancaster, PA: Technomic.

Kannapel, P.J., & DeYoung, A.J. (1999). The rural school problem in 1999: A review and critique of the literature. *Journal of Research in Rural Education, 15*(2), 67-79.

Lee, C.C. (2001). Culturally responsive school counselors and programs: Addressing the needs of all students. *Professional School Counseling, 4,* 257-260.

Metropolitan Life & Louis Harris Associates, Inc. (1997a). Percent of students who give the teachers in their school grades "A" or "B" for their teaching skills, by school location and student's race/ethnicity: 1996. *The Metropolitan Life survey of the American teacher, 1996, Part II. Students voice their opinions on: Their education, teachers and schools.* New York: Author. Retrieved on June 11, 2001, from http://nces.ed.gov/pubs/digest97/d97t075.html

Metropolitan Life & Louis Harris Associates, Inc. (1997b). Public school students' ratings of the quality of teachers and parental community support for their schools, by school location and students' race/ethnicity (in percent): 1996. *The Metropolitan Life survey of the American teacher, 1996, Part II. Students voice their opinions on: Their education, teachers and schools.* New York: Author. Retrieved on June 11, 2001, from http://nces.ed.gov/pubs/digest97/d97t074.html

Miller, B.A. (1995). *The role of rural schools in community development: Policy issues and implications.* Portland, OR: Northwest Regional Educational Laboratory. Retrieved on May 17, 2001, from http://www.nwrel.org/ruraled/Role.html

Morrissette, P.J. (2000). The experiences of the rural school counselor. *Professional School Counseling, 3,* 197-207.

Morrissette, P.J. (1997). The rural school counselor: A review and synthesis of the literature. *Guidance and Counseling, 13,* 19-23.

National Center on Addiction and Substance Abuse (CASA) at Columbia University. (2000). No place to hide: Substance abuse in mid-size cities and rural America. New York: Author. Retrieved June 22, 2001, from http://www.casacolumbia.org/usr_doc/23734.PDF

National Center for Education Statistics. (1996a). Mathematics proficiency of 4th grade students, by selected student and school characteristics: 1992 and 1996. *National assessment - Findings from the National Assessment of Educational Progress.* Washington, DC: Author. Retrieved May 28, 2001, from http://www.nces.ed.gov/surveys/ruraled/tables/NAEP_Math4.asp

National Center for Education Statistics. (1996b). Mathematics proficiency of 8th grade students, by selected student and school characteristics: 1992 and 1996. *National assessment - Findings from the National Assessment of Educational Progress.* Washington, DC: Author. Retrieved May 28, 2001, from http://www.nces.ed.gov/surveys/ruraled/tables/NAEP_Math8.asp

National Center for Education Statistics. (1998a). Average compensation (in 1997 constant dollars) received by full-time school teachers, by selected school characteristics: Summer 1993 and school year 1993-94. *Schools and staffing survey, 1993-94 (Public School Teacher Questionnaire).* Washington, DC: Author. Retrieved June 15, 2001, from http://www.nces.ed.gov/pubs98/condition98/c9857d03.html

National Center for Education Statistics. (1998b). Enrollment in public elementary and secondary schools, by race/ethnicity and locale: Fall 1998. *Common core of data survey.* Washington, DC: Author. Retrieved June 15, 2001 from http://www.nces.ed.gov/surveys/ruraled/tables/Race_Ethnicity.asp

National Center for Education Statistics. (1998c). Number of public school districts, by locale code (CCD) and state: 1998. *Common core of data survey.* Washington, DC: Author. Retrieved May 28, 2001, from http://www.nces.ed.gov/surveys/ruraled/Tables/SDU_Locale.asp

National Center for Education Statistics. (1998d). Number of public school students, by locale code (CCD) and state: 1998. *Common core of data survey.* Washington, DC: Author. Retrieved May 28, 2001, from http://www.nces.ed.gov/surveys/ruraled/Tables/Students_Locale.asp

National Center for Education Statistics. (1998e). Reading proficiency of 4th grade students, by selected student and school characteristics: 1992, 1994, and 1998. *National Assessment of Educational Progress, NAEP 1998 report card for the nation and states.* Washington, DC: Author. Retrieved May 28, 2001 from http://nces.ed.gov/surveys/ruraled/tables/NAEP_Read4.asp

National Center for Education Statistics. (1998f). Reading proficiency of 8th grade students, by selected student and school characteristics: 1992, 1994, and 1998. *National Assessment of Educational Progress, NAEP 1998 report card for the nation and states.* Washington, DC: Author. Retrieved May 28, 2001, from http://nces.ed.gov/surveys/ruraled/tables/NAEP_Read8.asp

National Center for Education Statistics. (1998g). Reading proficiency of 12th grade students, by selected student and school characteristics: 1992, 1994, and 1998. *National Assessment of Educational Progress, NAEP 1998 report card for the nation and states.* Washington, DC: Author. Retrieved May 28, 2001, from http://nces.ed.gov/surveys/ruraled/tables/NAEP_Read12.asp

National Center for Education Statistics. (1998h). Writing proficiency of 4th grade students, by selected student and school characteristics: 1998. *National Assessment of Educational Progress, NAEP 1998 writing report card for the nation and states.* Washington, DC: Author. Retrieved May 28, 2001, from http://nces.ed.gov/surveys/ruraled/tables/NAEP_Write4.asp

National Center for Education Statistics. (1998i). Writing proficiency of 8th grade students, by selected student and school characteristics: 1998. *National Assessment of Educational Progress, NAEP 1998 writing report card for the nation and states.* Washington, DC: Author. Retrieved May 28, 2001, from http://nces.ed.gov/surveys/ruraled/tables/NAEP_Write8.asp

National Center for Education Statistics. (1998j). Writing proficiency of 12th grade students, by selected student and school characteristics: 1998. *National Assessment of Educational Progress, NAEP 1998 writing report card for the nation and states.* Washington, DC: Author. Retrieved May 28, 2001 from http://nces.ed.gov/surveys/ruraled/tables/NAEP_Write12.asp

National Center for Education Statistics. (1999d). Public elementary and secondary students, schools, pupil/teacher ratios, and finances, by type of locale: 1996 and 1997. *Digest of education statistics.* Washington, DC: Author. Retrieved June 15, 2001, from http://www.nces.ed.gov/pubs2000/digest99/d99t089.html

National Center for Education Statistics. (1999e). *Teacher quality: A report on the preparation and qualifications of public school teachers.* Washington DC: Author. Retrieved on July 11, 2001, from http://nces.ed.gov/pubs99/1999080/index.htm

National Center for Education Statistics. (2000a). Age of public schools based upon years since construction of the main instructional building(s), years since most recent major renovation, and functional age of the school, by school characteristics: 1999. *Survey on the condition of public school facilities: 1999.* Washington, DC: Author. Retrieved May 28, 2001, from http://www.nces.ed.gov/surveys/ruraled/tables/Age_of_Schools.asp

National Center for Education Statistics. (2000c). Percentage of children in grades 3-12 with parents who were very satisfied with various aspects of the school their child attends, by selected family characteristics: 1993 and 1999. *National Household Education Survey (NHES), 1993 (School safety and discipline component) and 1999 (parent interview component).* Washington, DC: Author. Retrieved May 28, 2001, from http://www.nces.ed.gov/pubs2000/coe2000/section6/s_table60_1.html

National Education Association. (1998). *Status of public education in rural areas and small towns – A comparative analysis.* Washington, DC: Author. Retrieved April 12, 2001, from http://www.nea.org/publiced/rural.html

Perroncel, C.B. (2000). *Getting kids ready for school in rural America.* Charleston, WV: AEL, Inc. Retrieved April 12, 2001, from http://www.ael.org/rel/rural/abstract/perroncel.htm

Peterson, G.J., Beekley, C.Z., Speaker, K.M., & Pietrzak, D. (1998). An examination of violence in three rural school districts. *Rural Educator, 19*(3), 25-32.

Reynolds S., & Hines, P.L. (2001). *Vision-to-action: A step-by-step activity guide for systemic educational reform* (6th ed.). Bloomington, IN: American Student Achievement Institute.

Shaffer, L.S., & Seyfrit, C.L. (1999). *Rural youth and their transitions and pathways connecting school and work: A white paper.* Retrieved April 12, 2001, from http://www.nsf.gov/sbe/tcw/events_991104xw/start.htm

Sher, J.P. (1995). The battle for the soul of rural school reform: Can the Annenberg Rural Challenge turn the tide? *Phi Delta Kappan, 77*(2), 143-148.

Sherman, J.D. (1992). *Falling by the wayside.* Washington, DC: Children's Defense Fund.

Sherwood, T. (2001). *Where has all the 'rural' gone? Rural education research and current federal reform.* Washington, DC: The Rural School and Community Trust. Retrieved June 14, 2001, from http://www.ruraledu.org/ruralgone.pdf

Smith, P. (1999). "It's déjà vu all over again": The rural school problem revisited. In D.M. Chalker (Ed.), *Leadership for rural school: Lessons for all educators* (pp. 95-110). Lancaster, PA: Technomic.

Stern, J.D. (1994). *The condition of education in rural schools.* Washington, DC: United States Department of Education, Office of Educational Research and Improvement, Programs for the Improvement of Practice.

Synder, T.D., Hoffman, C.M., & Geddes, C.M. (1999). *Digest of education statistics, 1998* (DOE Publication No. NCES 1999-036). Washington, DC: U.S. Department of Education, National Center for Education Statistics. Retrieved June 20, 2001, from http://nces.ed.gov/pubs99/digest98/

Theobald, P., & Mills, E. (1995). Accountability and the struggle over what counts. *Phi Delta Kappan, 76*(6), 462-466.

Theobald, P., & Nachtigal, P. (1995). Culture, community and the promise of rural education. *Phi Delta Kappan, 77*(2), 132-135.

United States Department of Commerce, Bureau of the Census. (1998). Percent of high school dropouts (status dropouts) among persons 16 to 24 years old, by sex and race/ethnicity, and by metropolitan status: October 1998. *Current population survey, October 1998, unpublished tabulations.* Washington, DC: Author. Retrieved June 14, 2001 from http://www.nces.ed.gov/surveys/ruraled/tables/Dropouts.asp

U.S. General Accounting Office. (1996). *School facilities: American's schools report differing conditions* (GAO Report No. GAO/HEHS-96-103). Gaithersburg, MD: Author. (ERIC Document Reproduction Service No. ED397508)

Vissing, Y.M. (1998). *Homeless children: Addressing the challenge in rural schools* (Report No. EDO-RC-98-1). Charleston, WV: ERIC Clearinghouse on Rural Education and Small Schools. Retrieved June 20, 2001, from http://www.ael.org/eric/digests/edorc981.htm

Vissing, Y.M. (1996). *Out of sight, out of mind: Homeless children and families in small-town America.* Lexington: University Press of Kentucky.

Additional Resources for Classroom Use

Martin, Transforming School Counseling: A National Perspective (pp. 148-153)

1. Burnham, J.J. & Jackson, C.M. (2000). School counselor roles: Discrepancies between actual practice and existing models. *Professional School Counseling 4*, 41-49.

   This study compares what school counselors are actually doing to what has been suggested by leaders in the field.

2. Sears, S. J. (1999, January). Transforming school counseling: Making a difference for students. *NASSP Bulletin*, 47-53.

   The rationale for the Transforming School Counseling Initiative and how it will influence the role of school counselors is discussed.

3. Schmidt, J.J. (1998). *Counseling in schools: Essential services and comprehensive programs* (3rd ed.). Boston: Allyn & Bacon.

   This text for school counselors, psychologists, teachers, and educational administrators explains the importance of school counselors and how counselors and schools can provide services effectively. Presented is an overview of the school counseling profession, including the components of a comprehensive program of services and the current legal, ethical, and professional issues that are important to school counselors. Other topics include the history of the school counseling profession, the varying roles of the school counselor, and student appraisal.

House and Sears, Preparing School Counselors to be Leaders and Advocates: A Critical Need in the New Millennium (pp. 154-162)

1. UCLA School Mental Health Project web site http://smhp.psych.ucla.edu/

   This web site, which contains extensive resources, is cited here as a source of ideas for school counselors who wish to broker services and establish partnerships with social agencies and community organizations.

2. Wesley, D. (2001, Fall). The administrator-counselor team. *The Journal of College Admission Counseling*, 7-11.

   A solid administrator-counselor relationship is needed if both are to achieve their goals. This article discusses the importance of each professional to the other's success.

3. NCREL Pathways to School Improvement web site http://www.ncrel.org/sdrs/

   North Central Regional Educational Laboratory (NCREL) is a nonprofit organization dedicated to helping schools—and the students they serve—reach their full potential. Their Pathways to School Improvement web site is a comprehensive resource for those interested in school improvement. The site provides information on at-risk students, family and community, technology in education, and leadership.

Hanson and Stone, Recruiting Leaders to Transform School Counseling (pp. 163-168)

1. Hart, P., & Jacobi, M. (1992). *From gatekeeper to advocate: Transforming the role of the school counselor*. New York: College Entrance Examination Board.

   This text presents a strong argument for the pivotal role of school counselors in raising the achievement of ethnic minority and low-income students. Several problems and issues facing school counselors in today's schools, specifically those that align school counselors with the achievement gap between low SES Latino and African American students and their more affluent White peers, are identified. A new vision for school counseling that calls for training and preparation of school counselors for leadership of reform efforts is outlined. School counselors and counseling programs are challenged to be accountable in terms of the learning and achievement outcomes of students.

2. House, R.M., & Martin, P.J. (1998). Advocating for better futures for all students: A new

vision for school counselors. *Education, 119,* 284-291.

This article describes how the role of counselors must change to include social advocacy as a primary component. Counselors must work as change agents and advocates for the elimination of systemic barriers that impede academic success for all students. The primary role of school counselors who serve as assertive advocates is to create opportunities for all students to define, nurture, and accomplish high aspirations. Thus, school counselors become catalysts and leaders focused on removing the institutional barriers that continue to result in an achievement gap between poor and minority youth and their more advantaged peers.

3. Hilliard, A., III. (1991). Do we have the will to educate all students? *Educational Leadership, 49,* 31-36.

This article challenges educators to examine the beliefs they hold about children and their ability to learn. Once schools are untracked, it is necessary to turn attention to the delivery systems. However, cooperative learning, multiculturalism, decentralization, and technology are not enough. Educators must truly want to see each and every child develop to the best of his or her ability. This fundamental belief system must fit the new structures that are being created in order to support students to become successful learners.

Hayes and Paisley, Transforming School Counselor Preparation Programs (pp. 169-176)

1. McAuliffe, G., & Eriksen, K. (Eds.) (2000). *Preparing counselors and therapists: Creating constructivist and developmental programs.* Alexandria, VA: Association for Counselor Education & Supervision.

This book for faculty and supervisors preparing counselors and therapists for their work is aimed at both those students who are training to be counselor educators and those who are already preparing counselors. The text provides information on constructivist teaching and learning principles, designing constructivist programs, examples of best practices, and conclusions for the field.

2. American School Counselor Association web site http://www.schoolcounselor.org

The American School Counselor Association (ASCA) is a worldwide nonprofit organization based in Alexandria, Virginia. Founded in 1952, ASCA supports school counselors' efforts to help students focus on academic, personal/social, and career development so they not only achieve success in school but are prepared to lead fulfilling lives as responsible members of society. The web site contains multiple resources on the new model for school counseling, program development, and national standards.

3. American Counseling Association web site http://www.counseling.org

The American Counseling Association is a nonprofit, professional and educational organization that is dedicated to the growth and enhancement of the counseling profession. ACA helps counseling professionals develop their skills and expand their knowledge base by providing leadership training, publications, continuing education opportunities, and advocacy services to its members. This web site provides numerous resources and links related to the field and practice of counseling.

Jackson et al., Inducting the Transformed School Counselor Into the Profession (pp. 177-185)

1. Johnson, L.S. (2000). Promoting professional identity in an era of educational reform. *Professional School Counseling, 4,* 31-41.

In this article, professional identity of school counselors is addressed in terms of the need for reconceptualization of role by revisiting their stated purposes, functions, and relationships within the school setting/system. Focusing on how the school counselor effectively improves learning is identified as a critical factor for achieving professional legitimacy. The author provides a practical three-phase initiative to promote professional identity in an era of transformation.

2. Brott, E.B., & Myers, J.E. (1999). Development of professional school counselor identity: A grounded theory. *Professional School Counseling, 2,* 339-348.

Brott and Myers explored professional identify formation relative to school counselors. The purpose of this research was to arrive at a grounded theory of professional identity development and to conceptualize the role of a school counselor's personal interactions as formative experiences in identity development. This article is helpful for conceptualizing the "how" of furthering professional identity development as trainees enter the roles defined by new vision models.

3. CAREI (2002). *Transforming school counseling initiative, final report.* Retrieved July 15, 2002, from http://education.umn.edu/carei/Reports/TSCI_Final.pdf

This document provides a final evaluative report of the Transforming School Counseling Initiative. Within the document, induction is discussed as a necessary part of transformation. An overall discussion of the implementation of the initiative provides greater understanding for the need for induction and the manner in which professional identity can be transformed.

Musheno and Talbert, The Transformed School Counselor in Action (pp. 186-191)

1. Kapaes, J.T., & Whitfield, E.A (Eds.). (2001). *A counselor's guide to career assessment instruments.* Columbus, OH: National Career Development Association.

This book is designed for busy counselors who need quick reviews of the career development and assessment instruments available for school-aged children and adults. The book reviews 56 separate instruments using a standard format that includes Description, Use in Counseling, Technical Considerations, Computer-Based Versions, Overall Critiques, and References. Also included is a chapter that discusses recent developments in computer-assisted career assessment.

2. The Education Trust web site
http://www.edtrust.org

This web site describes the work of The Education Trust, a nonprofit organization that works for the high academic achievement of all students at all levels, kindergarten through college, and supports efforts to close the achievement gaps that separate low-income students and students of color from other youth. Education Watch Online is featured on the site. It includes The Trust's new national and state database, which is a user-friendly, interactive source of national and state data on achievement patterns by race and class. Education Watch Online is the latest in ongoing efforts to provide useful information for educators, policy makers, and the public. This site also includes a description of the six university sites that have been involved in the national Transforming School Counseling Initiative.

3. The ERIC/CASS web site
http://www.ericcass.uncg.edu/

The ERIC Counseling and Student Services Clearinghouse (ERIC/CASS), one of the original ERIC clearinghouses, was established in 1966 by Dr. Garry R. Walz at the University of Michigan. Its scope of work includes school counseling, school social work, school psychology, mental health counseling, marriage and family counseling, career counseling, and student development. Topics covered by ERIC/CASS include: (a) training, supervision, and continuing professional development; (b) counseling theories, research methods, and practices; (c) the roles of counselors, social workers, and psychologists in all educational settings at all educational levels; (d) career planning and development; (e) self-esteem and self-efficacy; (f) marriage and family counseling; and (g) counseling services to special populations such as substance abusers, pregnant teenagers, students at risk, and public offenders.

Hines, Transforming the Rural School Counselor (pp. 192-201)

1. ERIC Clearinghouse on Rural Education & Small Schools web site
http://aelvis.ael.org/eric/rural.htm

This site contains the Rural Directory, a listing of rural education resources, information from forums and chats dealing with rural issues, and access to ERIC digests on rural education issues.

2. National Rural Education Association web site
http://www.nrea.net/

Members of the National Rural Education Association include rural school administrators, teachers, school board members, regional service agency personnel, researchers, business and industry representatives, and others interested in rural education issues.

3. Pulling Together: R & D Resources for Small Schools web site http://www.ncrel.org/rural/

This site contains a collection of research and development resources for rural educators, such as related web sites, publications, training programs, model programs, and services.

4. National Data for Studying Rural Education web site http://www.ed.gov/databases/ERIC_Digests/ed383518.html

This ERIC digest, which describes datasets of the National Center for Education Statistics (NCES) that are related to rural education, discusses potential uses of NCES data and offers practical tips for accessing these data.

*The College of Education
of The Ohio State University presents*

THEORY INTO PRACTICE DIGITAL

The **complete** *Theory Into Practice* on a CD-ROM

A scholar's dream come true, *TIP-Digital* contains, on a single CD-ROM, 40 years of The Ohio State University's education journal, *Theory Into Practice* (1962-2001). Every theme issue, thousands of articles, on a broad range of education-related topics, can be easily accessed on this convenient disk.

Each of the 179 issues of *Theory Into Practice* is organized around a theme and features multiple perspectives and scholarly, yet accessible, discussions of current and future concerns in education. Edited and written by leading thinkers and practitioners in their fields, many of these theme issues are used in classes year after year as their message remains relevant indefinitely.

Whether you are a teacher, student, professor, administrator, or librarian, *TIP-Digital* will work for you:

For researchers
- Original page layout
- On-screen magnification
- Quality hard copies
- Great research capabilities
- Themes listed for fast access

For college courses
- Dynamic supplement and research tool for students
- Incorporates technology into higher education classrooms
- Fits snugly into student backpacks
- Major discount for quantity copies

New Prices

For individuals
CD only	$50.00/copy
CD + 1-year paper subscription	75.00/copy

For students
CD only	$25.00/copy

For libraries/institutions (includes site license)
CD only	$100.00/copy
CD + 1-year paper subscription	140.00/copy

Annual subscriptions to *Theory Into Practice* journal: $42.00, individuals; $68, institutions.

With MasterCard or Visa, you can order direct by email: tip@osu.edu; phone: 614-292-3407; fax: 614-292-7020, or mail check (made payable to The Ohio State University/*TIP*) to: *Theory Into Practice,* 341 Ramseyer Hall, 29 W. Woodruff Avenue, Columbus, OH 43210

See the *TIP* **web page** to read about more theme issues and award-winning articles: www.coe.ohio-state.edu/tip

Perspectives on Scholarly Misconduct in the Sciences
Edited by John M. Braxton

For almost two decades, cases of research misconduct have attracted the attention of both the academic community and the lay public. Such attention raises a fundamental question: Who holds responsibility for detecting, deterring, and sanctioning misconduct?

Perspectives on Scholarly Misconduct in the Sciences addresses this question by focusing on such topics as the social control of misconduct by the lay public, the congressional response to misconduct, the role that scientific associations and societies might play in deterring misconduct, the nature of policies and procedures universities have implemented to halt misconduct, how the graduate school socialization process can foster or deter academic malfeasance, and the response of individual academics to wrongdoing.

The book presents a framework for self-regulation, analyzes responses of universities to misconduct, and provides a workable definition of misconduct. It then looks at university-industry research collaboration as a potential source of wrongdoing and at legal issues associated with wrongdoing, finally setting forth a research agenda for studying misconduct.

Now revised and considerably expanded, this book began as a popular special issue of the *Journal of Higher Education*. *Perspectives on Scholarly Misconduct in the Sciences* is a valuable resource for scholars, university and college administrators, public policy makers, and officers of professional and academic societies interested in the development of policies to prevent scholarly misconduct.

272 pp. 6 x 9 13 tables
$50.00 cloth
0-8142-0815-0

at bookstores or
The Ohio State University Press
773-568-1550
www.ohiostatepress.org

It doesn't stand for "complimentary"

Most photocopying, reprinting or e-mailing of articles from trade journals, magazines, newspapers and Web sites without permission is against U.S. copyright law. Even if it's just for internal distribution.

Every year companies find out the hard way, spending tens of thousands of dollars to settle a single case. One company paid over $1 million because employees photocopied ordinary journal articles for their files.

Why take chances? Discover the easy way to protect your organization from noncompliance risks. Call today for your FREE, no-obligation Copyright Compliance Kit. See how very easy it is to copy right!

> **Order your FREE Copyright Compliance Kit today.**
> **Contact a CCC Marketing Representative**
> **at 978-750-8400**
> **marketing@copyright.com**

Copyright Clearance Center, Inc
222 Rosewood Drive
Danvers, MA 01923
copyright.com

For Product Safety Concerns and Information please contact our EU
representative GPSR@taylorandfrancis.com
Taylor & Francis Verlag GmbH, Kaufingerstraße 24, 80331 München, Germany

www.ingramcontent.com/pod-product-compliance
Lightning Source LLC
Chambersburg PA
CBHW081423230426
43668CB00016B/2336